Presidential Conflict in Côte d’Ivoire

Presidential Conflict in Côte d'Ivoire

Governance, Political Power, and Social Justice

T. Y. Okosun

LEXINGTON BOOKS
Lanham • Boulder • New York • London

Published by Lexington Books
An imprint of The Rowman & Littlefield Publishing Group, Inc.
4501 Forbes Boulevard, Suite 200, Lanham, Maryland 20706
www.rowman.com

Unit A, Whitacre Mews, 26-34 Stannary Street, London SE11 4AB

British Library Cataloguing in Publication Information Available

Library of Congress Cataloging-in-Publication Data

Names: Okosun, T. Y., author.
Title: Presidential conflict in Côte d'Ivoire : governance, political power, and social justice / T.Y. Okosun.
Description: Lanham, Maryland : Lexington Books, 2017. | Includes bibliographical references and index.
Identifiers: LCCN 2017050064 (print) | LCCN 2017049351 (ebook) | ISBN 9781498566568 (electronic) | ISBN 9781498566551 (cloth : alk. paper)
Subjects: LCSH: Presidents—Côte d'Ivoire—Elections—2010. | Contested elections—Côte d'Ivoire. | Côte d'Ivoire—Politics and government—1993- | Côte d'Ivoire—Economic policy. | Gbagbo, Laurent, 1945- | Ouattara, Alassane D., 1942-
Classification: LCC JQ3386.A95 (print) | LCC JQ3386.A95 O56 2017 (ebook) | DDC 966.68053—dc23
LC record available at https://lccn.loc.gov/2017050064

∞™ The paper used in this publication meets the minimum requirements of American National Standard for Information Sciences Permanence of Paper for Printed Library Materials, ANSI/NISO Z39.48-1992.

Printed in the United States of America

Pour la Côte d'Ivoire, bon courage (For Côte d'Ivoire, all the best).

Contents

Introduction

This book examines the conflict between Presidents Laurent Gbagbo and Alassane Dramane Ouattara of Côte d'Ivoire, which occurred between November 2010 and April 2011. The conflict, conditioned by complex elements within Ivoirian history, politics, culture, and internal struggles (class, ethnic, and religious), quickly developed into a national and international concern. While the conflict was specifically nestled within Côte d'Ivoire's delicate connections with France (its former colonizer), it was also of interest to the Western world, always seeking to guarantee its security, self-interests, and natural resources (raw cocoa and coffee in the case of Côte d'Ivoire). The conflict was a desperate struggle between two top leaders in Côte d'Ivoire. They fought and sought to entrench either autocratic dictatorship, or to define the nation toward a civil society that is sustained with some measure of democracy which respects universalizable rules of social and political engagement.

During the conflict, both presidents used various tactics in view of achieving their subjective and political goals. McCauley (2017), for instance, points out that in terms of conflict in Côte d'Ivoire (among other nations he considered) political leaders often manipulate ethnicity and/or religious sentiments to achieve their goals. Unfortunately, the use of preexisting ethnic, religious, and negative political sentiments drove a fragmenting wedge between Ivoirian leaders and citizens. That wedge deepened distrust among citizens already experiencing fragmentation from previous Ivoirian historical periods.

On the surface, the presidential conflict appeared to be an altercation between two highly politically privileged and powerful individuals. Nevertheless, the conflict was a symptom of much deeper problems festering at the local and national levels. It boiled over because President Gbagbo refused to leave office even after the reported higher percentage of Ivoirians who voted chose Ouattara as their new president. Several groups, including the United Nations (UN), governmental entities (African Union, henceforth AU, and the Economic Community of West Africa, henceforth ECOWAS), and independent African and Western groups who monitored the elections declared Ouattara the winner (UN Security Council 2011). Considering that Côte d'Ivoire emerged from a civil war in 2002 (Kouadio 2009) and that the nation was still in the middle of a restive condition in 2010 (UN Security Council 2011), it was clearly under standable that fear about the emergence of fresh hostilities as a result of the presidential conflict was real.

The conflict as it occurred was a complex socio-political, socio-economic, socio-religious, and emotively charged interpersonal/intergroup dynamic, which appeared juxtaposed to an existing simmering national tension (social and political unrest). Before the presidential conflict occurred, the fomentation of anger from laborers, students, the military, and others who felt disenfranchised in various ways resulted in social unrest culminating in two coups. One occurred in 1999 led by General Robert Guéï, which successfully toppled President Konan Bédié, and the other occurred in 2002 led by Guillame Soro, which did not quite topple President Laurent Gbagbo but resulted in the 2002 civil war (Kouadio 2009). These events, as they occurred, pointed to internal concerns about mounting governance and political improprieties, social inequalities, and the absence of a consistent and functional national social justice scheme.

Thus, this book is sustained by the notion that the intricate web of events which triggered the presidential conflict and the subsequent adverse effect on governance, political power, and social justice are located within pre-defined political elite advantages and privileges. In addition, these advantages and privileges were entrenched in seasoned, dominant, inflexible, and subjective ideological perspectives about deservingness and undeservingness nestled in widespread national perceptions of ethnicity, religion, class, and socio-cultural configurations. In other words, during the presidential conflict, the political struggles between ruling elites spurred on the already visible social disintegration which trapped the nation in confusion. The obvious measures of mounting social challenges were high poverty, insecurity, distrust, inequalities, and other critical social conditions experienced by the Ivoirian population. These challenges, which developed in the mid-1990s, were not just the outcome of contemporary socio-political activities but the brewed culmination of deeply embedded behaviors and actions that track back to Ivoirian colonial, post-colonial, and neo-colonial history.

This book examines and explores an aspect of this complex presidential conflict and its impact on governance, political power, and social justice. The style of the book follows a historical critical analytic approach. This helps with constructing a useful picture of the overall crisis, allowing for a critical and analytic evaluation of governance behaviors and actions through three specific periods of Ivoirian history.

During the conflict, the behavior and actions of the two conflict presidents demonstrated various ways in which they used their governance and political power. For instance, the book focuses on how both presidents responded to ballooning internal strife (over wages and calls for democracy); how they dealt with pending national development issues (healthcare, education, food shortages, and calls for social justice); how they dealt with concerns regarding deteriorating civil society; how they responded to concerns regarding human rights violations; and how they responded to appeals from the international community calling for good-faith negotiations to end the strife.

This book has nine chapters. Chapter 1 covers initial considerations regarding the presidential conflict. Chapter 2 presents a historical picture which explores the pre-conflict scenario in view of the conflict. Chapter 3 focuses on the presidential conflict through three distinct periods: the larger Ivoirian history, the specific Ivoirian history in view of the conflict presidents, and the immediate post-conflict Ivoirian context. Chapter 4 employs several theoretical perspectives to chart a diverse analytic explanation of the presidential conflict. Chapter 5 explores the conflict through the lens of social cubism, a very specific ethno-territorial conflict analysis model. Chapter 6 explores the different dimensions of dictator behavior. Chapter 7 presents and discusses a new theory (vapid insatiability) as a useful tool for explaining dictator behavior specifically within the West Africa/Africa context. Chapter 8 looks at the adverse impact and implications of the conflict in more detail, and chapter 9 discusses a conflict transformation model relevant to the Africa context, and ends with some interactive prescriptions. The book concludes with a discussion on the usefulness of heeding lessons from history.

Chapter One

Initial Considerations

This book emerged following a high interest in West African governance and political challenges and their intersection with various levels of complicated social issues. A visit to Côte d'Ivoire in the summer of 2010 led to the somber conclusion that the agitations and unrest in the country, at that time, were partly the result of Ivoirians' demand for actual democratic representation on one hand, and their struggle to establish a civil society sustained by social justice on the other. However, it was not enough to try to explain democracy and social justice issues in isolation from the political context. An extensive literature review initially revealed that the import of political power in Côte d'Ivoire was somewhat disconnected from democratic aspirations and concerns about social justice issues. It naturally made sense to explore the conflict between presidents Gbagbo and Ouattara in view of the implications it may have for political power, governance, social justice, democracy, and other issues.

Conflict at the highest political level has serious socio-economic and socio-political consequences. In much of the continent of Africa, understanding such a conflict is extremely useful because of the desperate need for deeper and more nuanced explanations and suggestions of possible solutions. Deeper explanations may also provide a platform for thinking or re-thinking future prescriptive options useful for conflict prevention.

Unfortunately, in some African nations, multiple adverse conditions are often constructed and sustained at the highest political levels. Some of these challenges include disinterest in good governance, functioning civil society, and infrastructural developments or improvements that are beneficial to all citizens. In some national contexts, powerful government leaders often fail to develop policies that encourage job creation, advances in healthcare options (many of these leaders, in fact, go to Western nations for medical treatment), and discourage democratic and social justice behavior. Instead of just articulating a historical contour of the presidential conflict, it is useful to intersect several historical periods, and from that analysis explore a new theory and a new conflict transformation model that may help with future explanation and direction when dealing with high-profile leadership conflict in West Africa.

CÔTE D'IVOIRE: THE PAST THROUGH 2011

The radical disjuncture between a once successful Côte d'Ivoire (from the 1960s–the early 1980s) and a now fragile Côte d'Ivoire (of the 1990s–2011) is difficult to imagine, let alone explain. Kouadio (2009) points out that the world which Felix Houphouët-Boigny, the first president of Côte d'Ivoire (1905–1993), constructed with varied coalitions and heterogeneity was shattered by Konan Bédié, General Robert Guei, Laurent Gbagbo, Guillame Soro, and many other power-hungry elite Ivoirians. These individuals did not understand how to create or sustain such important interactive coalitions between the rich and poor, various ethnic groups, and much more.

Because of the disintegration of the fragile socio-political context resulting from Houphouët-Boigny's death in 1993, it was inevitable that governance and political power issues would come to dominate Ivoirian social experience. As these issues increased in magnitude, elite political leaders' dissatisfaction with each other and social injustices resulting from political improprieties began to increase. Prior to the conflict between presidents Gbagbo and Ouattara, Côte d'Ivoire was already steeped in critical political crises, which for the most part presented challenges to those in power and their governance system. The emergence of the conflict between the two presidents was an additional burden on already existing political, economic, and social woes.

Therefore, the focus throughout this book is on how President Gbagbo's and President Ouattara's actions shortly before and during the presidential election in Côte d'Ivoire increased governance, political power, and social justice problems. However, before evaluating and discussing the impact of their actions, a preliminary exposition of their raucous relationship during the three periods of Ivoirian history is necessary.

Background and Relationship

The presidential conflict of Gbagbo and Ouattara revolved around intricate political, social, and economic challenges in Côte d'Ivoire. In pre-colonial West Africa (Diop 1987), Côte d'Ivoire was part of a large empire that dominated the Western part of Africa. Even though there were several ethnic and language groups, a king kept a tight rein on each group, yet allowed them independence as long as they were loyal and supported the kingdom with contributions.

Eventually the area composed of Côte d'Ivoire and Burkina Faso was colonized by the French nation (Weiskel 1980). French ownership of this colony was validated by the Berlin Conference of 1884, which established most parts of the continent of Africa as European possessions (De Leon 1886). While efforts to secure and dominate land and resources were in progress, colonization psychology insisted on getting Africans to internalize the French European ethos. The French ethos, much like other European ones, dichotomized significance and deservingness. In the structure of deservingness, the French viewed themselves as superior and special, and relegated the Ivoirians to inferiority and undeservingness. Although early Ivoirians resisted colonization (O'Sullivan 1993; Oloruntimehin 1993; Weiskel 1980), this dichotomy will became an important signature in post-colonial, independent, and contemporary Côte d'Ivoire (Mudimbe-Boyi 2009; Mudimbe 1992).

Moreover, even though the pre-colonial region, which included Côte d'Ivoire, was vibrant with traditions and coherent social systems, with political, religious, and economic worldviews (Diop 1987), the French colonial system simply disregarded and disrupted Ivoirian socio-cultural and past resplendence. For instance, travels and scholastic activities which converged in learning centers such as Timbuktu to the West, and Sudan (Nubia), Egypt, and Ethiopia (Axum) to the East (Diop 1974, Karenga 2002) were disregarded in favor of the European colonial agenda. Eventually, the Ivoirians internalized the French ethos and ways of life. This of course was advantageous to the French, but was devastating to Ivoirians. This colonial context would consequently haunt them for a very long time.

In contemporary Côte d'Ivoire, Ivoirian leaders and Ivoirians have faced critical challenges with regard to governance and fluid socio-political stability. Several scholars (Ayittey 2011; Moyo 2009; Obama cited in Dinan 2009; Ayittey 1992) argue that when dealing with critical current African issues such as governance, political leadership, conflict, violence, wars, and social development, the colonial and neo-colonial factors should be less emphasized. Instead, emphasis should be placed on current decisions and actions of corrupt political leaders and social elites. This perspective is both useful and interesting and requires a brief discussion here.

For instance, in North America D'Souza (1995), Herrnstein and Murray (1994), and Rushton (1995) use the intelligence argument to disconnect North Americans from historical culpability and connective responsibility by arguing that contemporary socio-economic arrangements ought to be judged by how intelligently people manipulate social conditions to their advantage. It follows that when African Americans speak about their disadvantaged conditions in relation to the history and implication of slavery, Jim Crow

Laws, Neo–Jim Crow laws (see Alexander 2010), and other social arrangements, these authors and their adherents insist that the focus should be on the present and not on historical deprivations and harmful actions.

This means that African Americans should only focus on the present, and no matter how history and collective negation trump their transformation, no linkages should be made of their struggle and challenges to hundreds of years of slavery, oppression, and past and present Jim Crow laws. A similar argument is found among some post-apartheid white, and even some Indian South Africans who still insist on blaming current conditions on Black South African behaviors and actions while nicely disregarding approximately 350 years of punitive, corruptive, and excruciating European colonization, segregation, apartheid, and dehumanization of Africans (Terreblanche 2002).

The point here is that, whereas Western paradigms often link their present to their past and vice versa, this practice is not preferred for others, especially Africans. This is what prompted Randal Robinson (2000) to examine the fragile condition of contemporary African Americans. For Robinson, African Americans are not only linked to Africa, but are specifically linked to European Americans by the actions of slavery, Jim Crow, and all the dehumanization that followed. Robinson worries that their increasing abandonment, along with the opinion that insists African Americans forget the past, discredits their powerful economic and social contributions (slaves for almost 215 years) to the United States. His solution is simple: keep the past and present connected and jump-start suffering and current African Americans with reparations. When asked, Terreblanche (2002) and Robinson (2000) would insist that tying any nation to its past, be it colonial or neo-colonial, is crucial if contemporary conditions are to be elucidated and properly understood.

It follows from the forgoing view that there are two global psychological histories. The first one is a cleaned-up history of all culpability for colonization and slavery and postulated as "positive history." This "cleaned-up psychological history" has implications for both the descendants of those who were involved in colonial and slave trade activities (Descendants #1), as well as for the descendants of those colonized and enslaved (Descendants #2). The second psychological history is loaded with humiliation, grief, and gloom. As for the two descendant groups, this second history is either easily erasable or not erasable at all. What is clear though is that Descendants #1 do not welcome or prefer the second history because it links them to the implications of colonies and the history of the slave trade. In addition, since Descendants #1 have never experienced the negative impacts of colonization and slavery, it is much easier to negate the second psychological history and insist that members of Descendants #2 simply forget the past and deal with their present. This simple but cruel tactic allows for guiltless blame of members of Descendants #2 as the sole architects of their own problems. Conversely, Descendants #2 cannot escape the devastating impacts of the second psychological history because they are forever connected to colonial, exploitative, and slavery actions, which fundamentally infected and still affects much of their behaviors and actions.

Of course, the argument that insists on just focusing on the present completely disregards the significance of historical continuity and the power of colonial psychology, which dehumanized colonized and enslaved populations from several angles, including but not limited to social, cultural, political, military, geographic, environmental, and religious dimensions. Moreover, as historical events unfolded, this negative transformation gradually became devastating to Ivoirians in many ways, notably in terms of the internalization of divisive propensities. In Côte d'Ivoire, much as in other African contexts, colonization succeeded in manipulating Ivoirians to become desensitized against some of their cultural experiences, corporate philosophies of life, and their ability to function and work collaboratively for their own self-determination. So that in just a hundred years or less, Ivoirians had moved away from their once-coherent corporate traditions developed over centuries to adopt French mystique and various versions of Eurocentric lifestyles.

It is useful to further point out that even though the French championed *liberté, égalite, et fraternité* (liberty, equality, and fraternity) as indispensable elements of true self-determination, in practice and during the colonial era they only defended these principles for their own benefit. Even within France, the aristocrats and the elite, a group which spanned Europe and which Karl Marx eventually collectively called the "bourgeois," viewed themselves as distinctively different from the rest of the mostly poor European citizenry. France's disconnection from its own principles of liberty, equality, and fraternity is telling when, for instance, Haiti (one of France's colonies in the Americas) appealed to these principles and requested independence from colonial bondage. The numerous requests were denied, and the Haitians had to fight their way to liberation and independence in 1804 (Ott 1987).

As colonization peaked in Côte d'Ivoire, French colonial schools became the norm, but this would clash with the vibrant indigenous systems, which still taught children traditional languages and cultures at home. Eventually, some creative Ivoirians (notably Houphouët-Boigny) created the space to organize and demand independence from France. The independence from France in 1960 became the impetus for constructing a new kind of geographic space named Côte d'Ivoire (the English-speaking world calls it the Ivory Coast).

Some of the challenges, notably perceptions about preferred forms of governance, would underlie latent tensions in the 1960s and 1970s. These latent tensions would manifest into open disagreements and political strife in the 1990s through to 2011. What became significant throughout post-colonial and independent Côte d'Ivoire appeared to be that governance and political power were being used to construct a pathway for henchmen and the elite to place themselves in extremely powerful and privileged positions. From the 1960s to the 1990s, only a few individuals (about 320 of them) were involved in the management of governance, political, economic, and other Ivoirian systems (Tessilimi 1984).

Since independence in 1960, much of Ivoirian society still mostly lives in socially and economically challenging conditions (Grootaert, Demery, and Kanbur 1996). The successive governance system following colonial methods helped those in power and the upper class to set up privileges, which in turn adversely affected most Ivoirians. Even though Côte d'Ivoire became the largest producer of cocoa on the globe, the planting and harvesting of the product mostly depended on the labor of poor immigrant farmers (Skogseth 2006). As well, the massive cocoa trade mostly yielded tremendous economic advantage to Western buyers and speculators, but translated into child labor and low revenue for poor Ivoirian farmers (Macguire 2011). In addition, judging from the level of poverty across the nation, even the overall revenue generated from the cocoa trade appeared guaranteed for elite privileges and advantages rather than for national development across the board. Ironically, when raw cocoa, rubber, coffee, and other products from Côte d'Ivoire arrive in Europe and other Western nations, they are processed into all kinds of capital-generating products with benefits for those citizens.

Similarly, though Ivoirians were economically successful in the 1960s, by the 1970s the governance system appeared to favor France and the importation of processed and manufactured goods from the West. This addictive dependency weakened what may have been Côte d'Ivoire's golden chance to develop massive self-sustaining productive capabilities. Unfortunately, the early internalization of dependency on France and imported goods by Ivoirian governance systems as solutions to internal development issues created challenging conditions. These challenges include the Ivoirian political leaders' struggle to maintain allegiance to France and deal with internal strife, while also increasing the subjective appetite for imported goods. To increase and sustain national revenue, the political elite insisted on the increase of internal agricultural productivity (raw goods for export to the West). Unfortunately, this diminished internal creativity in terms of developing self-sustaining systems. While Côte d'Ivoire increased agricultural productivity and revenue using poor citizens and immigrants as farmers, it inadvertently kept poverty and inequalities high. Increasing poverty and social unrest raised levels of agitation, apathy, and distrust of successive governance system to effect substantive political, economic, and social justice transformation (see Araoye 2012).

Consequently, increased political and social challenges in Côte d'Ivoire from the mid-1990s until 2010, when the conflict between presidents Gbagbo and Ouattara leaped onto the Ivoirian and global scene, appeared to be rooted in poor governance strategies that evolved shortly after independence in 1960. This is the point that Amondji (1986) sustains, adding that the problem of the construction of social injustices in Côte d'Ivoire began during colonization specifically because the French did not particularly care about enacting a functional scheme of distributive justice.

This means that during colonization, Ivoirians were not able to nurture their traditional system of protecting each other into a model of distributive justice on which to base their post-colonial and emerging new social and political system. Even after independence, instead of encouraging the first Ivoirian leaders toward inclusive democracy (a naturally occurring phenomenon in traditional Ivoirian society), the French focused instead on ensuring that the popular, powerful leader and friend, Houphouët-Boigny, would guarantee the flow of cocoa and other natural resources to them in Europe. Fortunately and surprisingly, the only integrative social justice system that occurred came from the creative effort of Houphouët-Boigny, who invented a sort of Afrocentric interactive political system (Kouadio 2009) which held the nation together from the early 1960s until his death in 1993.

After Houphouët-Boigny's death, the gradual disjunction between governance and its service to Ivoirian citizens led to increased political agitation. Clearly, independence did not bring about strong interest in some of the democratic yearnings for civil societies that were fomenting changes in Europe and elsewhere on the globe in the 1960s, 1970s, and 1980s. Instead, in Côte d'Ivoire independence and the years that followed became a period when the political elite and their allies honed their manipulation of the government platform and used it to build individual and subjective legacies. Some elements of the legacies included entrenching themselves as the only political leadership option, as well as extending their presence in governance indefinitely.

Tessilimi (1984) points out that from the beginning of independence (1960–1990s) Côte d'Ivoire's political system was managed by just 320 elite individuals. This was clearly an autocratic system that basically micromanaged the entire nation and sought no input from citizens. After more than fifteen years in office, it was clear President Houphouët-Boigny was a dictator, albeit a benign one. As well, the nature of the governance system did not allow for a fundamental or concerted response to social justice across the board. Instead, Houphouët-Boigny became a benign micromanager who gradually manipulated Ivoirians to depend on the political elites as their sole provider and protector. This signifies that even though Côte d'Ivoire was actually more productive and economically self-sustaining in its early years of independence from France, it neither had long-term sustainable nor democratic socio-economic, and socio-political networks and systems aimed at the benefit of everyone.

It is ironic that during the 1970s through the 1980s, members of the Ivoirian political elite developed certain areas of the country that served their interests while neglecting remote areas. This was clearly colonial thought at work in Ivoirian leaders. Like many African elites, Ivoirian political elites enjoyed open access to Europe, the United States, and parts of the world that offered tremendous pleasure and opportunities. But because of collective political shortsightedness, the best practices from those parts of the world where they basked in tremendous pleasures were never translated back to Côte d'Ivoire or other African nations. Ultimately, questions began to arise about the nature of the Ivoirian governance system and whether or not these leaders were actually interested in democracy, civil society, justice, and fairness for all citizens.

By the late 1980s, perceptions about political power in Côte d'Ivoire were hinged on the idea that powerful individuals who gained access to political power adopted and exhibited patterned behaviors. Two such behaviors are that (1) the Ivoirian president and his supporting team stayed in power indefinitely, and (2) that these same individuals have unfettered access to national monies often used for subjective interests. This socio-political socialization created an internalized system of entitlement that normalized itself all across Côte d'Ivoire.

In this scenario, what used to be positive African traditions (inclusive of corporate behavior and distributive justice) and common sense which encouraged the use of best practices from other parts of the world were systematically neglected in favor of a micromanaged and subjective governance system. Since there were no resources reaching Ivoirians in remote parts of the nation, many of them sought opportunities elsewhere, especially moving to the larger city of Abidjan. Access to common resources such as good roads, housing, good sanitation, and healthcare were limited in remote parts of the nation. Somehow the Ivoirian dictatorial style of governance had inadvertently created a socio-political and socio-economic mess. By the arrival of the civil war in 2002, Ivoirians were no longer able to divest and diversify themselves away from the version of dictator governance constructed and popularized by its powerful political elite.

It is useful to add that political power had become an important experience and tool vehemently sought after because of the advantages it created. Ethnic and ethno-territorial issues soon materialized that forced Ivoirians to become suspicious, angry, distrustful, aggressive, and violent against each other. It is hard to pinpoint exactly when it all began, but by 2002 Ivoirians had divided themselves into bitter polarities. By 2010, especially with the emergence of the presidential conflict, it became clearer that the raging animosity between groups made violent confrontation more attractive than conflict negotiation.

By the late 2000s thousands of Ivoirians began leaving the country because of mounting social injustices such as human rights and dignity violations, increased inequality (see Aka 2006), ethnic antagonism, and governmental opposition. Because of these conditions, the direct contestation for power in the nation increased, with some individuals offering to reclaim Côte d'Ivoire and "restore" it to civility and others promising "democracy" and inclusive governance. The problem with these contestations and promises was that right up to 2010 no model of "real" transitional democracy existed in Côte d'Ivoire from which to draw lessons. Conversely, the nation was replete with examples of individuals seeking political power by making promises they never kept. The picture was not any different in many other African nations where individuals seeking political office emerge with claims to transform governance but end up creating more problems (Ayittey 2011). That has been the case in Nigeria, Liberia, Sierra Leone, and Zimbabwe, to name a few nations.

The tragic nature of a dictatorial governance system is that it promises opportunities on one hand but delivers very little on the other. For Côte d'Ivoire, the civil war that broke out in 2002, during Gbagbo's presidency, was an indication of a long oppression and exclusion of most citizens from opportunities, forcing Ivoirians into restive and insecure conditions (Kouadio 2009). For years, the Ivoirian political elite held the Ivoirian system up as self-determining, nationalistic, and more progressive within West Africa. Even though this may be true, the same Ivoirian elite had tactically entrenched layers of social inequalities and discord into the nation. As a result, a large number of Ivoirians faced social and economic challenges, with many finding themselves as refugees in foreign countries, while others used the period to regroup and to think about national reconstruction.

Within this confusion, Laurent Gbagbo became Ivorian president in 2000, and it was during his presidential tenure that civil strife began with a nearly successful coup led by Guillame Soro. After the civil war in 2002, the United Nations helped to broker a referendum. The idea was for President Gbagbo to stabilize the country and call for elections in 2005, but this never occurred. Several negotiations through internal and international efforts finally led to the 2010 democratic elections.

Consequently, Gbagbo, the champion of democracy who had published several scholarly books on governance and democracy (see Gbagbo 1982, 1983), had gradually but tactically reenlivened dictatorial and ethnic sectarian conditions while being president. Although these are speculations much beyond the scope of this book, it is possible that Gbagbo used his published works on democracy to get into national governance, understanding that he was really just an autocratic dictator. It may also be the case that he was naïve in distinguishing between theorizing on democracy and its actual practice, so that while in power his democratic theoretical ideal failed to have significance in the face of powerful contenders, hence his political instinct to consolidate his power as an autocrat and dictator.

Consequently, Gbagbo's refusal to leave office, even after many Ivoirians, the United Nations, and independent monitoring bodies clarified and ratified that Ouattara had won the 2010 elections, led to the complicated standoff between Gbagbo, who chose to stay and declared himself ongoing president, and Ouattara, who stood by his own victory and declared himself president. Ultimately, the presidential conflict would have tremendous implications for governance, political power, and social justice in Côte d'Ivoire.

Conflict Period and Assumptions

Presidents Laurent Gbagbo and Alassane Ouattara were in conflict between November 2010 and mid-April 2011. Three periods were examined in order to get a broader understanding of the conflict: (1) the pre-conflict period, (2) the conflict period, and (3) the post-conflict scenario. An extensive exploration of pertinent literature helped with the construction of a broad historical picture. The literature also helped with evidence to understand the conflict's implications for governance, political power, and social justice.

Four assumptions undergird the study in this book. The first is that the Gbagbo-Ouattara presidential conflict was something expected on both sides because of deeply internalized subjective expectations. These expectations focused on personal benefits at the expense of those governed, specifically the lower stratum of Ivoirian society. Judging from the conflict history of Côte d'Ivoire (McGovern 2011; Tiabas 2009), the second assumption holds that because political power is inflexible and nonnegotiable, it was expected that the two presidents, who were deeply socialized in autocratic and dictatorial dynamics, would not capitulate to each other except through the use of violence.

The third assumption holds that because the conflict was occurring at the very top of the political realm (between two presidents), its impact would be far reaching, including social, economic, religious, and political damage to all Ivoirians. The fourth assumption is that the terms "conflict," "governance," "political power," and "social justice" are generally accepted global terminologies such that using them for the Côte d'Ivoire context (though used with contextual nuances) carried the same general meaning and significance as elsewhere on the globe.

Leadership and Conflict Transformation in Africa

Increasingly, African nations, specifically fragile ones without useful natural resources, are of less interest to powerful and technologically advanced nations focused on self-interest and crucial domestic and international activities. For instance, this tactical dismissive approach denied Rwanda during its 1994 genocide any assistance (Straus 2006). Ironically, the Congo region, with its numerous raw materials, also suffers the same dismissal. Considering that the conflict in Congo (still ongoing) has led to the death of millions of people (Stearns 2011), there may be other reasons for the dismissal of even resource-rich nations specifically from the African continent. Most recently, the Sudan conflict, which lasted for years and peaked as another African genocide, was also similarly dismissed (Hamilton 2011). Even the solution to break Sudan (an oil-rich nation) into two nations has exposed more of the core disinterest in sustaining fragile nations, such as South Sudan. Because of the absence of internal and global collaboration to support fragile African nations to build thriving civil and progressive nations, most of them struggle to survive under powerful military and/or extremely corrupt autocratic civilian dictators.

In most cases, even with a few thriving African nations, the impoverished conditions within many of these nations have remained unchanged or have in some cases increased (see Sachs 2005; see also Bond 2006). Sub-Saharan Africa, especially the West African region, is notorious for its powerful dictator rulers. The Côte d'Ivoire scenario between 2010 and 2011 was specifically sensitive and dangerous because it had two individuals—one the incumbent president and the other incoming president—sustained by a "democratic" win of the presidential election, fighting over political power. They both claimed the presidency and both assumed power, one governing from the presidential palace, and the other from a hotel for a period of six months, until violence erupted to settle the matter.

The standoff between the two presidents helps to underscore one of the most troubling problems in West Africa, and perhaps all of Africa, namely the disconnection of previous from current political elites when they gain power and become a new governance system. In this scenario, the new government generally throws out the old government's positive efforts, but ironically sustains the negative behaviors, such as corruption, nepotism, embezzlement, total disregard for civil society, disregard for the rule of law, and a complete disconnection from democratic behavior. This governance behavior occurs to some extent in other parts of the world, but its manifestation in West Africa/Africa dislodges the continuity of positive development, making national and regional progress elusive. This negating behavior is probably partly due to the intense resentment that each group (constitutive of ethnic, religious, class, and political differences) harbors against the other.

Terminology

In contemporary global arrangements very basic definition of common terms, especially when used in a specific context, is useful for an easy read through a book. For the Côte d'Ivoire context, the following terms appear frequently: conflict, governance, political power, social justice, elite, and civil society.

"Conflict" is generally viewed by several scholars (Schellenberg, 1996; Jeong 2000; Bush and Folger 2005; Moore 2003; Folger, Poole, and Stutman 2005; Pruitt and Kim 2004) as incompatibilities of perceptions between contending parties. Conflict has categories: intra/interpersonal, intra/intergroup, and intra/international. These categories make it easier for practitioners to know how to approach conflict analysis in view of a useful transformation plan/model.

However, no matter where conflict is occurring, its analysis must take into consideration a vast array of dynamics. In addition, even though contexts determine conflict scenarios, conflict has both positive and negative implications, and the general psychology of aggression, face-saving, determined inflexibility, and posturing are indications that survive across social and cultural contexts. The presidential conflict in Côte d'Ivoire was a multilayered conflict. It had interpersonal, intergroup, and international components, and was intractable. Intractable conflicts almost always have aggression or violence.

"Governance" is the collection of actions performed on behalf of citizens by any government or corporate entity. The term governance often refers to institutional or organizational stability, but in this book, it points to what any group in political leadership should really focus on when providing services to citizens in any nation. For instance, Carver (2001) clarifies the notion of governance in relation to the work of the board of directors of an institution. The board of directors is often nestled between the owners of a system or institution and the chief executive officer. This relationship is important for three reasons: (1) the board of directors is in consistent and ongoing dialogue with owners of an institution, in order to be clear on expectations for the specific results required; (2) the board of directors expresses those expectations in documented standards for success; and (3) the board of directors always checks to ensure compliance with the standards. This all means that in the governance dynamic, the board's central concern is connection to the owners, institutional policymaking, and constant monitoring for policy compliance.

In the case of Côte d'Ivoire, the idea of governance is similar to the "board of directors'" arrangement. The people of Côte d'Ivoire are the owners of the nation, and the president is the chief executive officer. In this governance grid, political representatives comply with the owners' desires, standards, and policies.

"Political" power in this book is the prerogative given to political representatives by citizens, and has the implication and significance of collective power. The owners, that is, citizens of a nation, always own and discharge political power through elected representatives. These representatives, as in the case of Côte d'Ivoire, receive the mandate to enact useful and transformative rules and policies on behalf of all Ivoirians.

"Social justice" is harder to define because it has been associated at various points of world histories with socialism. Social justice defined here is a collective, voluntary responsibility that responds to the unavoidable needs (justice, equal representation, inclusion, access, equal opportunity, etc.) of all citizens, but specifically the less advantaged members of any social context (Novak and Adams 2015; Young 2011; Okosun 2009; Barry 2005; Novak 2000; Rawls 1971). This voluntary contextual response is determined and understood as a specific aspect of justice, often called distributive justice, which aims for the fair distribution of common life-sustaining resources to all citizens. These common resources should be accessible to everyone in a given social context (Rawls 1971; Barry 2005).

However, social justice also features in the larger global context when it considers the globe as one geographic social space or as a global community. For the larger global context, specifically when two nations and/or regions (one affluent and the other truly disadvantaged) come up, social justice becomes a useful platform for discussion as to what is the right thing to do. This is easily understood when measuring, for example, global poverty and people's access to basic sustenance and resources such as food, water, medicine, shelter, and clothing. Thus, the use of the term in the Côte d'Ivoire context is in relation to all Ivoirians having access to equal opportunity and treatment, and the fair distribution of common resources, ethnicity, religion, and social class notwithstanding.

"Elite" is a common term that is generally popular across the globe. Following Mills's (1956) definition, it is a group (almost always) of a limited number of individuals who assume power, wealth, and privilege through constructed economic, political, class, and social differentiation. Although nuances are slightly different, the Ivoirian context informs upon the nature of elite privileges in much the same way as everywhere else on the globe. It has a self-selected group of individuals who enjoy tremendous benefits and access to special privileges, while simultaneously disregarding the rule of law, deemphasizing civil society and social justice, and insisting on sustaining autocratic and dictatorial conditions.

"Civil society" has become an important pursuit across the globe (Walzer 2009; Putnam 2009; Shils 2009). In this book, civil society manifests as a context of tranquility wherein good governance and the rule of law converge to sustain fundamental policies that are advantageous to everyone across the board. In civil societies, people can pursue their desires and goals without fear of interdiction or governmental or other abuses. Civil society mostly begins with restorative transformation, a process of restoring to an individual, a group, or a community that which was taken from them. This could be dignity, rights, access, resources, and so on. Moreover, civil society thrives through transformative justice, a process that encourages complete reorganization of harmful rules of engagement, behavior, and practices so that citizens' lives transition from worse-off to better-off conditions. Civil society is a democratic agreement of all citizens in a social context, where everyone pledges to protect each other come hell or high water.

Chapter Two

The Pre-conflict Scenario

The presidential conflict appears innocently simple and the temptation is to examine it as it is for the period in which it occurred. However, because the two feuding presidents are deeply connected to various experiences within past Ivoirian political history, this chapter discusses the pre-conflict scenario in relation to the presidential conflict.

CÔTE D'IVOIRE: THE PRE-CONFLICT PERSPECTIVE

Before Felix Houphouët-Boigny became president of Côte d'Ivoire in 1960, the French colonial presence was already deeply entrenched in the region. The French discovered various raw materials (cocoa, coffee, etc.) and took control of political, social, and economic life. This colonial presence created numerous challenges to Ivoirians. France entered Côte d'Ivoire in 1842, and shortly after, the Berlin Conference of 1884 ratified European occupation of Africa's coastline and extended the ratification to cover the effective occupation of Africa's interior in 1890 (De Leon 1886). France made Côte d'Ivoire a colony in 1893. Ten years after full colonization (1904), the French made Côte d'Ivoire part of the Federation Francaises d'Afrique L'ouest (Federation of French West Africa) (Anouma 2005; Mel 2005; Koffi 2010).

Frances's eventual domination of the region did not go unchallenged. The Baoulé, a highly sophisticated Ivoirian ethnic group with an advanced political and administrative system, put up extremely strong resistance against French incursion into Côte d'Ivoire (Ivory Coast: Pre-European Period 1988). Despite the resistance, the French took total control of the region and enjoyed relative comfort of control until the appearance of the amicable Houphouët-Boigny, a medical doctor and an agriculturalist. Houphouët-Boigny helped set up two important groups: the Syndicat Agricole Africaine

(SAA) and the Parti Democratique de la Côte d'Ivoire (PDCI). In 1944 he became head of the SAA, and in 1945, he was elected to the national assembly in Paris. These appointments increased his local and international profile. With his guidance, the SAA grew to become a platform to foment democratic rallies. Also his founding and direction of PDCI, Côte d'Ivoire's first democratic party, helped galvanize other less-known Ivoirians to join him to move Côte d'Ivoire toward freedom and independence from France in view of political self-governance (Anouma 2005). Eventually his democratic rallies and political activities led Côte d'Ivoire into a republic in 1958 and full independence from France in 1960. Houphouët-Boigny became its first president and stayed in power for thirty-three years until his death in 1993 (Mel 2005).

In 1958, two years before Côte d'Ivoire got its independence from France, Houphouët-Boigny successfully convinced Ivoirians and France that Côte d'Ivoire needed to remain within the French community. Houphouët-Boigny already anticipated that the success of the new Côte d'Ivoire would require collaboration and continued interaction with France. What he did not anticipate at the time was that France would use that connection to entrench itself as a powerful external influence in internal Ivoirian matters.

As with every deal, some Ivoirians were concerned about the relationship between Côte d'Ivoire and France. The concerns were that the relationship was illusory at best and an indication of neo-colonialism (Ottemey 2009). This is to say that something was fishy when internal leaders pitched tent with former colonial masters. This perhaps was the first signal that the new Ivoirian leader was setting up for a long sojourn in the presidency. In West Africa/Africa, the period between 1958 through 1968 was tumultuous. In Nigeria, for instance, a close neighboring nation, political leaders such as Tafawa Balewa (prime minister from 1960 to 1966) and Agui Ironsi (1966) were killed in violent coups. So for Houphouët-Boigny, it was a tactical move to link himself by way of his nation to France for military and other protective privileges in case things went awry.

After becoming the Ivoirian president in 1960, Houphouët-Boigny led Côte d'Ivoire through a successful economic and a somewhat peaceful political period, interrupted by two seldom-mentioned coups—one in 1963 and the other in 1972. Houphouët-Boigny gradually morphed from democratic ideals and aspirations to becoming a "benevolent" autocratic dictator (Mel 2005; Koffi 2010; Amondji 1986). It is particularly interesting that Houphouët-Boigny entered political office with strong democratic ideas, but ended up as a tactful benign autocratic dictator. This behavior was clearly a signal of how political socialization would entrench itself in the Ivoirian socio-political scene. Here, a glimpse of the initial foundation of the series of events that would overtake Côte d'Ivoire in the 1990s and onward emerges.

By the mid-1980s the price of cocoa fell and other internal economic challenges emerged (Mel 2005), and by the late 1980s agitation for popular and actual democracy gained traction. Houphouët-Boigny softened and legalized multi-party elections as well as opposition parties, allowing them space in the political electoral experience in 1990, thirty years into his dictatorial reign. It is possible that Houphouët-Boigny understood that he had become an autocratic dictator who assumed that democracy was best realized through the control of an enlightened "big" tough man. The other possibility may be that he finally gave in to multi-party elections because he realized that he had taken his style of political governance too far. Also, he may have been influenced to adopt a multi-party system, at last, after noticing that apartheid, one of the most brutal dictatorial systems in the world, had collapsed in South Africa.

Ironically, Houphouët-Boigny still won the election, defeating a young and inexperienced Laurent Gbagbo. Gbagbo was the only one who dared to run against him under his political party, the Ivoirian Popular Front (FPI). It is not clear whether the agitations of the clamor for political change in Côte d'Ivoire got to him, or that it was simply the end, but in 1993, just a couple of years after the 1990 elections, Houphouët-Boigny dies in office. President Houphouët-Boigny's death in 1993 brought an end to a tenuous thirty-three years of "relative" stability in Côte d'Ivoire (Attebi 2011; Gakunzi 2011; Ndiaye 2011; and Mel 2005). From 1993 onward, the nature of political governance in Côte d'Ivoire changed dramatically, moving from manageable economic and social stability to periods of increased agitation and disintegration.

Houphouët-Boigny was an astute politician who from the beginning consolidated his power by making sure that all religious and ethnic groups, including local rulers, were incorporated into his system of political governance. This means that he endeared himself to every group from the elites at the top to the poorest villagers and local chiefs at the bottom (Kouadio 2009). This form of shared but tactful consolidation of power may have been his secret to political governance.

However, beyond Houphouët-Boigny's charm, dictators all have something in common. They have ways of imposing fear and/or dependency on citizens. In many cases they use ephemeral material and immaterial promises to mesmerize and hook people to allegiance (see Acemoglu and Robinson 2006; see also Moore 1966). During Houphouët-Boigny's tenure in the presidency, it may be that he psychologically endeared Ivoirians to love, revere, and depend on him simultaneously. Because of this emotive allegiance, even the agitations and calls for actual democracy in the late 1980s were not powerful enough to sway most Ivoirians. They were too loyal and used to the status quo, and not ready to welcome an unknown newcomer, Gbagbo, to disrupt what they perceived to be national stability.

For those Ivoirians who felt they were doing well, change in political representation was not necessary. This group, which would be a combination of elite Ivoirians and all other privileged citizens, may have viewed Houphouët-Boigny's gesture of at least allowing a multi-party political platform a good enough move. But because of a socialized expectation of uninterrupted privileges guaranteed by Houphouët-Boigny, no further actions (especially of electing a new unknown) were needed. It is useful to note that President Houphouët-Boigny and all those who gained from his support were not ready to relinquish control of revenue from the world's largest exportation of cocoa. Electing an unknown individual, Gbagbo, with no political governing experience was dangerous.

Yet other explanations of Houphouët-Boigny's success are possible. It might also be that Ivoirians had reached a point where their society was so stratified that the majority of the have-nots muddled in poverty and undereducation had no creative ways of challenging and demanding change. This could be the case where they simply did not know how to go about taking political power away from Houphouët-Boigny. In other words, even though they may have wanted a more egalitarian social arrangement, Ivoirian society was already fully rigged with dictatorial political arrangements which were beyond their knowledge and effort. Ironically, many members of the elite population with the knowledge and ability to do something for change were not eager to make changes because their privileges mostly came from the benign dictator, whom they were too glad to reinstate as president in 1990 despite his age, failing health, and longevity in power.

The final reason could simply be that none of the above ruminations are valid and that rich and poor Ivoirians alike simply trusted Houphouët-Boigny more than anyone else at the time (1990). This trust was hinged on Houphouët-Boigny being the founding father of the nation, a hegemonic stalwart linked to France (McGovern 2011), and the architect of several progressive socio-economic developments which made certain parts of Côte d'Ivoire (especially Abidjan) look, feel, and function like an African Paris. Also, his trustworthiness may have emerged for reasons linked to satisfaction, happy discontent, fear of the unknown, and reliance on the ability of the incumbent to deal with internal and external political forces. It could also be that such trust was based on Marxist false consciousness which led to an unusual acquiescence that the status quo was just fine, and that tampering with it may result in social, economic, and political fragmentation.

Even though Ivoirians respected Houphouët-Boigny because he was the founding father of Ivoirian independence, and contributed to political and economic changes in Côte d'Ivoire between the 1980s through the early 1990s (Koffi 2010), Gbagbo and other democracy activists show that he had become an autocrat who ran a form of addictive dictatorship until his death.

However, the series of national issues that eventually emerged were due to delay in enacting political reform.

As soon as the economic downturn in the mid-1980s began, Houphouët-Boigny introduced Alassane Ouattara into the Ivoirian political scene as an economic guru and commissioned him to fix the economic problems. Ouattara's austerity program angered Ivoirians (Kouadio 2009), but the changes he made did ease things up a bit. His success in calming economic agitation, and perhaps other internal maneuvering, led Houphouët-Boigny to appoint Ouattara as the prime minister of Côte d'Ivoire. This one action set up a series of discontentments on the part of Henri Konan Bédié and Gbagbo, causing them to redouble their efforts in terms of positioning themselves for coming political power struggles.

After Houphouët-Boigny's death, Henri Konan Bédié stealthily assumed the presidency in 1993 by yanking power from Ouattara, the prime minister who had been acting president of the nation while Houphouët-Boigny was ill. Laurent Gbagbo, who ran in the 1990 elections and lost, also embarked on a series of political and scholarly works in an effort to demonstrate the problem of autocratic dictatorship and the need for an actual democracy. Ouattara, unhappy with Bédié's move, retreated to consolidate his energy and efforts for a future return. The intense animosity between these three political elites and others launched Côte d'Ivoire into unprecedented political and eventually socio-economic instability.

The animosity against Ouattara began when Bédié was president of the Ivoirian Parliament from 1980 to 1993 and Ouattara was the Prime Minister of Côte d'Ivoire from 1990 to 1993 (Quenum 2011a). This interpersonal conflict between Houphouët-Boigny's anointed heirs, Bédié and Ouattara, now had to contend with an outsider, Laurent Gbagbo, clamoring that actual democracy was overdue in Côte d'Ivoire. For Bédié and Ouattara, a newcomer insisting on actual democracy would interrupt privileges and the continuity of Houphouët-Boigny's autocratic dictatorship.

So, the larger Ivoirian conflict and the struggle between political elites to control political power in Côte d'Ivoire evolved between 1980 and 1993. During this period, the interpersonal conflict between Bédié and Ouattara intensified and created socio-political challenges. Bédié's usurping of the presidency specifically weakened Ouattara's chances of immediately gaining access to presidential power (Quenum 2011a).

Consider that Ouattara was the vice president at the time of Houphouët-Boigny's death. This suggests that he would have been the natural heir to the presidency. In other words, it would have been politically responsible for Ouattara to finish up Houphouët-Boigny's term before new elections, but Bédié assumed the presidency through aggressive legal maneuvering. As socio-economic and political conditions worsened during Bédié's tenure as president, he was deposed in a 1999 coup masterminded by a disenchanted

General Robert Guéï, who was only in power for a few months. The interpersonal conflict between Bédié and Ouattara made it possible for Gbagbo to assume the presidency in 2000 after Bédié's and Guéï's tumultuous tenures as presidents from 1993 to 1999, and 1999 respectively.

There were other catalysts that helped fuel the conflict between the now contending triumvirate of Bédié, Ouattara, and Gbagbo. It is also at this point that ethnic and religious sentiments began to break through and infect political activities. But the series of events (decisions and policies) which led to the economic downturn of the mid-1980s highly contributed to the rageful political character of the period (Amondji 1986). Even though Côte d'Ivoire began to show signs of recovery from economic stress during this period, especially with the adoption of a structural adjustment program (introduced by Ouattara and external influence and which included currency devaluation), poverty continued to increase, especially in rural areas (Kakwani 1990). This was, of course, an indication of increasing national stress which was having noticeable impact on Ivoirians, especially those at the lower stratum.

It is not surprising that Gbagbo, a radical political activist, emerged to demand changes in Côte d'Ivoire. Gbagbo was concerned about the increasing gap between the Ivoirian elite intricately connected to France and the poor. Houphouët-Boigny imprisoned him for two years (from 1971 to 1973) for his oppositional activism. However, Gbagbo was fully convinced that the Houphouët-Boigny hegemonic problem could only be resolved through organized activism. In 1982, he launched his political party, the Ivoirian Popular Front (FPI) and was naturally made its leader in 1998, setting up a political platform to openly challenge Houphouët-Boigny and run for the 1990 elections (Koffi 2010; Djea 2009).

Interestingly, within this same period and across several parts of Africa, powerful discourses began to emerge on the consequences of colonialism and neo-colonialism blended with tragic internal hegemonic and dictatorial propensities (von Albertini 1982). The general consensus was that African political elite using colonial and neo-colonial mentalities were adversely affecting their internal political governance (Moyo 2009; Ayittey 1992). The idea of neo-colonialism emerged when African scholars began to suspect that the agents of their colonial past were still active on the continent through international policies which were adversely affecting many nations in Africa. This notwithstanding, many Africans elected to study in Western nations because the educational and other opportunities (labor, research, and well-being) were better organized and more attractive.

Moreover, it may have been difficult for Africans who studied in the West and returned to their respective nations not to transfer or impose foreign perspectives on their nations. They superimpose Western processes as the better option for quality and change in Africa. This means that when Africans brought their Western education back home, and unwittingly imposed them on public processes in their respective nations, they were participating in a form of neo-colonization that helped former colonizers continue their remote influence within Africa nations.

Conversely, Bédié, Ouattara, and Gbagbo all studied and worked in Western nations. Their behavior and actions exhibited a deep blend of internalized and inerasable colonial, neo-colonial, and Western perspectives. These perspectives clashed to foment social and other divisiveness that eventual led to national disintegration. Given such powerful Western influence, it is not surprising that Gbagbo mounted an anti-colonial and anti-neocolonial campaign to purge Houphouët-Boigny's neo-colonial dictatorial system in favor of a Western-style democracy in Côte d'Ivoire.

In addition, it is useful to mention that the behavior and actions of the Ivoirian political elites struggling for political power mirror the disjunction postulated by discourses on internal divisiveness in Africa. From Houphouët-Boigny's period all through to General Robert Guéï, the military general who overthrew President Bédié and installed himself as president in 1999, a pattern of inflexible political behavior materialized that echoed the mounting divisiveness. The sudden dominance of individual power struggles between increasingly inflexible and agitated political elites formed one of the dynamic sources of the conflict (Assalé 2009).

These intense elite power struggles not only had interpersonal implications, they also adversely affected the entire nation. Thus, the democratic revolution in Côte d'Ivoire from 1989 to 1995 (Sahi 2005), which included Gbagbo calling for multi-party elections and actually running against Houphouët-Boigny in 1990 and Bédié as president after the death of Houphouët-Boigny, became a charted course of political contention instead. Because of intense power struggle, an increasingly choatic nation emerged, going from a highly progressive context where economic and social expectations were fluid to a nation transposed with disintegration and violence (Koffi 2006).

A closer look at Henri Konan Bédié may be helpful in constructing his part in the larger Ivoirian crisis. Bédié was the president of the Ivoirian Parliament, placed there by Houphouët-Boigny in 1980. Upon Houphouët-Boigny's death he assumed the presidency. Bédié's specific announcement to the nation on the evening of Houphouët-Boigny's death was a signal of the beginning of what would become an intense, ongoing Ivoirian political crisis (Quenum 2011a).

Once in power, Bédié began to maneuver to stay in power indefinitely. He was drawing a page from the Houphouët-Boigny autocratic dictatorship manual. He restricted opposition parties, notably those led by Ouattara and Gbagbo, from participating in elections. His inflexible political action caused Gbagbo (who had challenged Houphouët-Boigny in 1990 and lost) and other opposition parties to boycott the 1995 election. Bédié's move to preclude opposition parties gave him full victory to move from interim to full president of the country (Koffi 2010; Assalé 2009).

Bédié become a powerful political player in Côte d'Ivoire (Koffi 2010; Assalé 2009; Baulin 2000; Bosson 1994) because all of his moves were made possible by his mentor, President Houphouët-Boigny. Between 1966 and 1977, Bédié's tenure as Minister of Finance and Economy got Côte d'Ivoire its highest economic success in the sales of cocoa and coffee. In 1977 Bédié moved to the World Bank as advisor to Robert McNamara (then president of the World Bank), while also serving as head of the Africa division of the bank. In 1980 he was elected to the Ivoirian parliament and was made its president. Following Article II of the Ivoirian Constitution, which he helped craft, he automatically became the heir to the president—should anything happen. Bédié stayed in this position until the death of President Houphouët-Boigny in 1993.

It is interesting that Bédié and Ouattara were brought into political office by Houphouët-Boigny and anointed into different but significant positions. That notwithstanding, a raging rivalry developed between them. This rivalry would become one of the sources of the emerging political conflict to dominate Côte d'Ivoire from December 7, 1993, when Houphouët-Boigny died in office, all through to the Gbagbo and Ouattara presidential conflict in 2010/2011. Because he had been in the parliament and had intricate knowledge of Ivoirian national laws, Bédié quickly used his new presidential power to exercise legal reform.

From 1995–1999 he reversed Houphouët-Boigny's "Open Door Policy" to introduce Ivoirité, which made access to presidential power and other rights and privileges only open to full Ivoirian citizens. Full Ivoirian citizenship required individuals to have Ivoirians as both parents. This new program, which was considered nationally divisive and extremely negating of northern Ivoirians, was Bédié's tactical way of excluding some of his rivals and their followers (most specifically, Ouattara) from any attempt at the presidency. It was also a move to prevent his opponents from enjoying other important rights and privileges in Côte d'Ivoire. Those vilified by the Ivoirité program were considered half-Ivoirians with no substantive rights (Kouadio 2009).

Consequently, Bédié's presidential reign from 1993 to 1999 was a period of intense social, political, economic, and ethnic polarization (Tiabas 2009; Kouadio 2009; Toha 2008). Because of the economic downturn in the late 1980s to the early 1990s Bédié acceded to the devaluation of the Ivoirian franc in 1994 (Tiabas 2009; Toha 2008). As well, Bédié's new Ivoirité law instantly marginalized much of the northern half of the country, many of them Muslims who contributed immensely to the nation's life and culture (Fofana 2007). The marginalization included ethnically different citizens and residents, specifically those who were children of past and ongoing migration from Mali, Burkina Faso, and to some extent other West African nations.

Moreover, because of the Ivoirité program, northern Ivoirians were subjected to interminable abuses culminating in the denial of Ivoirian national identity cards, passports, common socio-economic resources, and other important rights and privileges. Bédié's rise to power had simply created an impossible situation for the nation, throwing it into political turmoil and marginalizing large groups of Ivoirians. By 1998, cocoa and coffee prices had dropped down to their lowest value on the global market, forcing farmers to blockade the Abidjan seaport (Quenum 2011a). This was an important additional response to the mounting frustration with the political elite and their governance approach. Instead of creating policies that would further national cohesion and progress, Bédié acceded to the devaluation of Ivoirian currency and set up one of the most dangerous programs to destabilize Ivoirians and turn them against each other.

A number of expedient questions emerge at this point. Was Bédié being naïve about his actions, or did he believe that throwing the nation into chaos would be helpful in his quest to sustain an indefinite sojourn in the presidency as did his predecessor? Bédié was both naïve and subjectively vindictive. His tortuous political elitism did not allow space to anticipate that his erratic actions would dramatically affect the socio-economic and socio-political stability of the nation. Because of the unfortunate consequence of the Ivoirité program (part of his grand plan to entrench himself in the presidency), conditions became so bad that migrants from Burkina Faso had to flee for their lives (Skogseth 2006; IRIN 2005). Since many of these immigrants worked in the cocoa farms, their instability destabilized cocoa and coffee production and revenue. Ivoirité unleashed stifling ethnocentrism, nationalism, and toxic intolerance across the nation.

At the peak of the intolerance, it no longer mattered whether migrants had children who were actually Ivoirians because of birthrights, or had been in the country for more than half a century. What mattered was that political elites and their followers had found a potent way (the use of Ivoirité) to create instant advantages for themselves while simultaneously creating disadvantages for vilified Ivoirians.

It is useful to point out that the nation of Côte d'Ivoire was formed by precolonial groups that came from several parts of Africa and settled in the area. The Muslim Kong Empire, which was established by Juula, flourished until the 1890s when it was vanquished by Samori Toure, but its descendants are still around. The Abron Kingdom settled in Côte d'Ivoire after fleeing from the Ashanti of Ghana and is still around. Then a thriving Muslim population settled in Bondoukou, where commerce and Islamic scholarship attracted students from many parts of West Africa. The Baoule Kingdom was established by the Akan group who also fled from the Ashanti of Ghana. And then there were two Agni kingdoms formed by migrants who eventually made Côte d'Ivoire their home. It is worth mentioning that the Agni kingdoms were so independent and Afrocentric that even after Côte d'Ivoire got its independence from France, they sought to secede in 1969. Mostly based in the southeast of the country, they wanted a separate and meaningful African identity (Ivory Coast: Pre-European Period 1988).

Interestingly, even though these pre-colonial groups are the same diverse ethnicities that make up present-day Côte d'Ivoire, Bédié unleashed a negative and divisive differentiation program on his nation. As president, he was supposed to create national cohesion. Instead, he dismissed past and present intermarriages that formed contemporary Ivoirian families, and he failed to recognize that the movement and interactions of ethnic groups led to ethnic and religious diversity in Côte d'Ivoire as well as other African nations. Specifically, Bédié and his political team disregarded the history of Côte d'Ivoire and its vibrant diversity to institute the harmful Ivoirité program.

Consequently, Bédié's presidential tenure was characterized by tension, divisiveness, and national fragmentation (Koffi 2010; Quenum 2011a). His plan to stay in power in order to continue the legacy of autocratic dictatorship by antagonizing and restricting opposition parties demonstrated his contempt for civil society and political sanity. As discontent and anger over his behavior and actions increased, the move by Ouattara (once the Ivoirian Prime Minister, but in the eyes of Bédié, a Muslim, a northerner, and a half Ivoirian) to leave his International Monetary Fund (IMF) post and return to Côte d'Ivoire to run for the presidential office forced Bédié into manic rage. Ouattara's move to return to Côte d'Ivoire and challenge Bédié escalated the conflict between them (Quenum 2011a). Toward the end of his presidential tenure, and in the midst of increasing internal difficulties, the IMF and the World Bank, citing Bédié's government corruption and irresponsibility, cut off loan funds in 1999 (Baulin 2000).

From another interesting angle, Bédié's presidential tenure gives a glimpse into the nature of the extremely slim connection between Ivoirian political elites and their interest in sustaining social justice. Bédié attempted to reposition himself for the 2000 elections by touting his service to Côte d'Ivoire. He evoked an emotive shade that pointed to his thirty-five years of government service (Sibi and Bédié 1995). While Ivoirians were in desperate political and economic conditions, Bédié touts his achievement only because he wanted political continuity. Like his predecessor, and many other African leaders, Bédié developed an inflexible affinity to the privileges of the presidential position, and increasingly maneuvered to stay in power indefinitely. Even after he was overthrown by General Robert Guéï in the 1999 military coup (Quenum 2011a), he still tried in the 2000s to use his long national service credential to reenter the presidential office.

In the end, even though Bédié was overthrown in a military coup in 1999, he had succeeded in polarizing the nation (Tiabas 2009; Toha 2008). His institution of Ivoirité, his vilification of Ouattara as a non-Ivoirian of Burkina Faso nationality, and his move to discount Ouattara and others as unworthy of the Ivoirian presidency, all led to a divided nation formalized into discontented and negating camps. General Guéï, Bédié's nemesis, was no good either. Forcibly installing himself as interim president exacerbated the already tense and critical political condition.

Moreover, following the dictatorial patterns played out by Houphouët-Boigny and Bédié, Guéï's attempt to rig the election and impose himself on the nation as president snapped Ivoirians out of their reticence and patience. The people's massive protest forced Guéï out of office in 2000 and paved the way for the Gbagbo presidency. General Guéï's behavior and action of trying to manipulate his way into the presidential office demonstrated the level of corruption and disregard of democracy and civil society. Bédié and Guéï were not interested in instituting a civil society with democratic ideals wherein the rule of responsible and inclusive laws would service all Ivoirians. Instead, they mostly used their political power to go after personal gains and to oppress others they deemed undeserving.

As for Gbagbo, his rise to power and to the Ivoirian presidency was a mixed bag of challenges. His presidency was both a political victory at first (for himself) and for some others who thought true democracy had arrived. But his tenure as president eventually became a socio-political mess because it so much increased national stress (Agou 2010). The numerous crises that emerged during Gbagbo's presidency became a nightmare that divided the country and turned citizens into enemies (Tavares 2005; Toha 2008). For instance, socio-political instability in Côte d'Ivoire was linked to political improprieties with the specific period between 1959 and 1999 serving as the impetus of all the strife that followed (Tiabas 2009). This means that Houphouët-Boigny and his successor, Bédié, sowed the seeds that grew into the series of socio-political conflicts which Gbagbo inherited and that would increasingly plague Côte d'Ivoire until his ouster in 2011.

From yet a different angle, the larger Ivoirian crisis scenario became a *Legacy of Constraints* (Toubabou 2005). When the discussions of constraints arise in African nations, disadvantages are defaulted to the poor who make up a majority of these nations. In the case of Côte d'Ivoire, constraints are simply the series of measures that gradually expelled democracy and civil society and enthroned political rivalry, which enabled difficult socio-economic conditions. Even when President Gbagbo and the ruling team scrambled to appease the nation, and offered a program of socio-economic development, some Ivoirians wondered whether the whole thing was just an illusion (Toualy 2008). Concern about whether Gbagbo's development program was an illusion had traction specifically with regard to the increased adverse conditions experienced by masses of poor Ivoirians. Put differently, Gbagbo simply came to power to maintain an autocratic sojourn like Houphouët-Boigny and Bédié (Toubabou 2011).

In terms of building national coherence, Gbagbo's policies were problematic (Ba and Wade 2005). Gbagbo, the leader of the Presidential Majority (LMP) which was an alliance of Gbagbo's Popular Front of Ivory Coast (FPI), entered office with a democratic ticket in 2000, but by 2005 was manifesting symptoms of manic domination syndrome. Like Bédié, who prevented him and Ouattara from the presidency for a long time, Gbagbo was now in volatile interpersonal conflict with Ouattara, who had reconstituted himself and emerged to be a powerful political contender.

Gbagbo was also embroiled in smaller conflicts with other powerful contenders such as Bédié, Gueï, and Guillame Soro (the 2002 coup and civil war mastermind). These individuals also ran for the 2010 presidency but were less significant in terms of Ivoirian appetite for presidential choice. Nevertheless, the different conflictual engagements contributed to Gbagbo's manic rage to consolidate his political power. His agitation was increased when it became clear that Ouattara had been anointed by the Alliance of the Houphouetists (RHDP) (Quenum 2011a), a powerful group that promoted and sustained Houphouët-Boigny's "Open Door Policy" and interactive governance legacy.

Already in 2005, just a few years after he assumed presidency of Côte d'Ivoire, Gbagbo's sense of political governance was divisive and fueled national disintegration. Gbagbo gradually consolidated himself into an autocratic dictator with contempt for democratic rules (Ba and Wade 2005). This was unusual because Gbagbo's several books focused on democracy, civil society, and the need for national coherence, but some of his actions included the refusal to hold elections, ordering of airstrikes against Guillame Soro and his rebel group, and holding on to the presidency even after his mandate expired in 2005.

Gbagbo's legacy of contending for a democratic Côte d'Ivoire goes further back. Positioning for political power, the *Front Populaire Ivoirien* and Gbagbo put out a document in anticipation of changes in the nation in 1987. Gbagbo, a professor and a history academic, had carefully thought about the nature and implications of the Houphouët-Boigny presidency. He concluded simply that Houphouët-Boigny was an autocratic dictator deriving support for his power and protection from France and the Western world. In 1987, Gbagbo began his gradual march toward the presidency. He understood the significance and power of an organization, and since he did not like the idea of a dictatorial government, he formed a political system, the Front Populaire Ivoirien (FPI). He was mostly pointing to democratic ideas in his new system, while also laying out the foundation on how to democratically govern

Côte d'Ivoire. Gbagbo tested the strength of the FPI when Houphouët-Boigny allowed multi-party elections.

In terms of Gbagbo's perspectives on democracy, politics, civility, and freedom in Côte d'Ivoire, a decisive portrait emerged in a piece contributed by Mbem (2010). Mbem examined Gbagbo's intellectual and political work in detail. Two distinctively different Gbagbos emerged: one a theoretician, and the other a classic Ivoirian politician. Gbagbo's intellectual efforts were theoretical insights into an ideal world where democracy and civility are easily practiced. However, in the real world, specifically in Côte d'Ivoire, where ideals usually conflict with dynamic human divergences, Gbagbo's political stance and actions were troubling but not surprising.

Earlier, in 1982, Gbagbo offered a detailed book on the Ivoirian economy between 1940 and 1960. This is a comprehensive analysis detailing various economic activities in the given period, and perhaps Gbagbo's first attempt to create a critical discourse about Côte d'Ivoire and its relationship with France. In it Gbagbo argued that between 1937 and 1938, economic activities in Côte d'Ivoire picked up. He pointed out that the French colonists discovered cocoa beans, coffee, and other resources, and that though they experienced difficulties transporting these products because of World War II and maritime challenges, the colonists had found something extremely important and were not going to let go. Gbagbo added that the colonists had challenges bringing products into Côte d'Ivoire to sustain the resident colonists. He concluded that even though the French were deeply anchored in Côte d'Ivoire, they had also been weakened by World War II (Gbagbo 1982).

Gbagbo's point was that no matter how much the French colonial machine tried to dress itself up after World War II, especially because it was ransacked by Germany (and it had to concentrate its efforts on liberation and rebuilding), its colonial influence, efforts, and power were greatly reduced. The impact though of the colonial enterprise was still heavy on Gbagbo's mind as he asked whether Côte d'Ivoire is a decolonized country after twenty years of proclaiming independence (Gbagbo 1982, 201). He answered the question by insisting that French imperial activities were active in imposing successive reforms following the independence of Côte d'Ivoire. This means that Côte d'Ivoire's economic decisions post-1960 were still being manipulated by the neo-colonial logic of imperial France, which in turn was affecting internal politics and conditions within Côte d'Ivoire (Gbagbo 1982, 202).

In his 1982 book, Gbagbo makes himself part of the anti-neo-colonial scholars' group who detest interference from outsiders manipulating African, and in his case, Ivoirian destiny to their advantage. His point was also a direct shot at the government of Houphouët-Boigny, which he viewed as collaborating with France. Neo-colonization and imperialism in Côte d'Ivoire and in many other African nations had adverse effects (Kouadio 2006). They were viewed as meddling in internal affairs and a form of recolonization of Africa (Kouamouo 2007). However, the meddling with the internal affairs of some African nations by the United Nations, specifically in response to crises such as the Ivoirian crisis, is useful and necessary (Koulibaly 2009; Assouman 2006).

By 1983, African nations were filled with autocratic dictators who simply believed that they were the only ones who had the mandate to rule. In 1989, Gbagbo reenters the Ivoirian scene with another book chronicling his imprisonment from 1971 to 1973, his struggle against a dictatorial system, and his return to form a thriving political party that would challenge Houphouët-Boigny in the 1990 election. Gbagbo gave insight as to his democratic aspiration, and how he conceived the nature of political governance. At this point, Gbagbo was opting for a democratic scenario which was going to be inclusive of the diverse Ivoirian population, as well as conscious of the people's social conditions and plight (Gbagbo 1989).

Gbagbo followed his 1989 book with yet another book in 1991 after losing the first multi-party elections in Côte d'Ivoire in 1990 to the incumbent, Houphouët-Boigny. The focus of the book was a response to the significance of activism in view of freedom. The idea of freedom for Gbagbo was to wrest the governance of Côte d'Ivoire from a dictator who had been in power for so many years. His conception of freedom was also imagined for the general population of Côte d'Ivoire who would be free to become participants in Ivoirian political life. The book was a call to action, and an endorsement and a call for democratic liberties. In accordance with his philosophy and activism for democracy, he was the only one who dared to challenge and run against the autocratic dictator Houphouët-Boigny in 1990.

By 1995, Henri Konan Bédié had already been in office for about two years after having seized the presidency upon Houphouët-Boigny's death in 1993. In that year, Gbagbo adds a hint of hopefulness to the Ivoirian quest for democracy in his new book *The Time of Hope*. This was also Gbagbo's way of reminding Ivoirians that democracy was still possible and that it required work and activism to get there (Gbagbo and De Sumo 1995).

Gbagbo eventually became president in 2000, and after five years in office his presidency had generated many socio-economic and socio-political problems. Gbagbo continued to view his political regime as the only one that would introduce useful changes to Côte d'Ivoire. No matter how tenuous his reign became, Gbagbo kept manipulating the global community to support and continue to sustain his emerging dictatorial regime. Internally, he plugged into Ivoirité set in place by President Bédié, but was careful in the ways he used it. The Young Patriots and other groups were his Ivoirité surrogates.

In 2009 Gbagbo felt compelled to explain his case through publication (Gbagbo 2009). This book appeared as a surprise because in it he tried to point to the discourse of peace as something linked to democracy and prosperity. The book is very important because it gives insight into how Gbagbo viewed himself in a political governance position. Gbagbo was either delusional as he made his case for peace while the nation was in chaos, or he believed that the world would come to his side when he entered the arena of peace discourse. Unfortunately, from the beginning of his presidency up until the time of his 2009 book, his behavior and actions were autocratic, dictatorial, and contrary to the practices of peace, democracy, or prosperity. The book was one more indication of the contradiction between Gbagbo the scholar and Gbagbo the dictator.

At this point, some insight into Alassane Ouattara is in order. Ouattara's legendary profile is demonstrated by his service at the highest levels of national political and global monetary systems. He served Côte d'Ivoire as prime minister under Houphouët-Boigny between 1990 and 1993. In addition—despite the marginalization experienced in the hands of Bédié and Gbagbo—Ouattara, a northern Muslim, made it beyond all expectations to be the director from 1973 to 1975, and from 1988 to 1990 vice governor of the Banque Centrale des Etats de l'Afrique de l'Ouest (BCEAO)—Central Bank of French West African Nations (based in Paris). He also served from 1984 to 1988 as the director of the African Department and as counselor to the Managing Director of the IMF (Cissé 2007).

In 1990, during his tenure as vice governor of the BCEAO, Houphouët-Boigny invited Ouattara to serve as chair of the Interministerial Committee for Coordination of the stabilization and Economic Recovery Program in Côte d'Ivoire. His brilliance in getting the economy rolling once again earned him Houphouët-Boigny's anointing as the prime minister of the nation. He served in this position from 1990 to 1993, and because of Houphouët-Boigny's grave illness, Ouattara served as interim commander-in-chief of Côte d'Ivoire for the greater part of 1992–1993. When Bédié seized power after Houphouët-Boigny's death in 1993, Ouattara returned to the IMF to serve in the position of deputy director from 1994–1999.

Ultimately, Ouattara's November 7, 1990, appointment as prime minister of Côte d'Ivoire was a formal anointing by Houphouët-Boigny (Quenum 2011a). This was probably an indication that President Houphouët-Boigny was having second thoughts about Konan Bédié and his move to manipulate the constitution to his advantage. It is hard to say, but something exciting about Ouattara's appointment was the clear signal that Houphouët-Boigny needed someone with astute economic sensibility whom he could trust with the nation as he dealt with age-related issues and critical illness.

Moreover, despite Ouattara's northern and Islamic heritages, Houphouët-Boigny's "Open Door Policy" was inclusive of ethnic, religious, and other differences. Ouattara's participation in political affairs at the highest level was never a question. After Houphouët-Boigny's regime, being the son of an Ivoirian mother and a Burkina Faso father caused Ouattara and all northerners like himself some major difficulties. Ouattara's (2003) own scholarly piece gives insight into his view of Ivoirian social reality. He used his 2003 piece to respond to the nature of increasing poverty in Côte d'Ivoire. He examined the 2002 results of living standards and found that the nation was regressing in its response to poverty. Ouattara most probably focused on the issue of poverty because he wanted to highlight that the political governance system at the time was failing to respond to the crucial issue of distributive justice in the nation. *Les Bilans alimentaires de la Côte d'Ivoire 2001–2007* (Côte d'Ivoire & Food and Agriculture Organization of the United Nations 2008) gave credence to Ouattara's 2003 perspective showing decline. Ouattara also focused on the relationship between socio-political interaction and freedom (Touré 2008), and on ways to lift Ivoirian youth beyond their current conditions (Touré 2010).

In 1999, Ouattara left his IMF post in Washington, D.C., and returned to Côte d'Ivoire to prepare for the October 2000 elections. Ouattara became the leader of the Rassemblement Des Republicains (RDR)—Rally of the Republic—which was formed by Ouattara supporters. RDR was formed as a result of Bédié's antagonism against Ouattara and the removal of Ouattara supporters from the largely Bouale-dominated PDCI (Houphouët-Boigny's political party) government (Skogseth 2006).

In President Bédié's scramble to respond to and slow Ouattara's political threat, he found eleven pro-Ouattara political leaders, including four legislators, to be in contempt of his policy (especially Ivoirité). He accused them of socio-political activism (these individuals were simply siding with justice and fairness) and sent them to prison for two years beginning in November 1999. This drastic action was Bédié's way of guaranteeing a substantive sabotage of key political opponents most likely to help Ouattara in his bid for election to the presidency.

When Houphouët-Boigny ran for election to the National Assembly in 1946 under the Partie Democratique de Côte d'Ivoire (PDCI), he picked two individuals from the North (one of the Mossi ethnic group, and the other of the non-Mossi group), then called Upper Volta (Zolberg 1964), to support him. Northern Ivoirians are mostly Muslims with roots in Burkina Faso, Mali, and other neighboring North and Northwest African nations. The Muslims have a rich history in Côte d'Ivoire. They were there before European colonists came, and contributed robust intellectual and cultural content to Côte d'Ivoire (Fofana 2007). As part of the national character, it was senseless to create any negating program that affected them dramatically. In addition, because many ethnic groups make up the nature and character of Côte d'Ivoire (Ekanza 2007), it is impossible to view Bédié's Ivoirité as anything but divisive.

Bédié's Ivoirité had succeeded in sowing discord, but he had clearly overlooked the deeper interconnections that existed between most Ivoirians.

Even though divisiveness had created bitter antagonism, it was Gbagbo's re-introduction and use of Ivoirité as an additional polarizing tool that triggered the 2002 civil war in Côte d'Ivoire. That war was for the most part a political reform crisis, which had its origin in 1993 when Houphouët-Boigny died in office (Kouadio 2009). From that point on, Bédié, Guéï, and Gbagbo fueled and fed on a steady diet of political polarization.

In summary, Bédié consolidated his political power and refused to allow elections in 1995. General Guéï stepped in and removed him in 1999. Then General Guéï, seeking to be president by all means, refused to run under PDCI and formed his own party, Union Démocratique des Peuples de Côte d'Ivoire (UDPCI)—Democratic Union of the People of Côte d'Ivoire. He refused to leave the interim presidential position until a massive protest forced him out so that Gbagbo could take over in 2000. By 2009 Gbagbo had sunk the nation deeper into socio-political oblivion and increased national agitation and divisiveness undergirded by Ivoirité. Because ideologies have a way of gripping proponents to high levels of emotive rage, the Ivoirian political feud leaped from "electoral politics" to a realm where the Ivoirité program was normalized and used to dehumanize citizens (Kouadio 2009).

Ivoirité emerged in a complicated scenario. The background of its creation is located in the 1990 elections. During the elections, Gbagbo was the only challenger to Houphouët-Boigny, and he lost. His FPI mostly in exile in France was sustained by a powerful student-dominated Fédération Estudiatine et Scolaire de Côte d'Ivoire (FESCI)—Federation of Students and Scholars of Côte d'Ivoire. Somehow, increasing animosity between Gbagbo, his followers, and the PDCI (Houphouët-Boigny's party) led Ivoirians of the Kwa and Krou groups (Gbagbo is from the Krou ethnic group) to accuse the PDCI government of granting Ivoirian national identity cards to foreigners of northern origins to boost their 80 percent win and their 163 over 175 parliamentary control. The anger eventually exploded into a massive riot against the PDCI and the government in 1992 (Skogseth 2006).

Even though Gbagbo was hurting from his election loss in 1990 and from his arrest in 1992 for unruly activism against the PDCI, he somehow decided to link his political FPI party with President Bédié's PDCI. This was a complicated alliance, but it was designed to deal with the question of who was a "real" Ivoirian, hence eligible to political rights and privileges. The Ivoirité question was, therefore, an attempt to discern between different levels of "Ivoirian-ness."

For instance, it raised the question of whether the mostly Muslim Mande and Gour groups from the North who are also found in the South and who make up almost 23 percent of the population were to be viewed as real Ivoirians. Complicating the Ivoirian scenario was the inflexible position adopted by Bédié that the Boaule and Agni (of the Kwa group which escaped from the Ashanti in the pre-colonial period) were the only ones with political leadership capabilities (Skogseth 2006). As far as Bédié and Gbagbo were concerned, Ouattara was ineligible to be president because of what they perceived to be his semi-Ivoirian-ness. He was considered half Burkina Faso and half Ivoirian.

No matter how Ivoirité became expressed, its acceptability and use as a xenophobic and ethnically divisive program helped in disconnecting Ivoirians from each other. It also helped in disconnecting them from the pursuit of social justice, a form of justice which responds to the fair distribution of common resources, and encourages the formation and sustenance of civil society. As well, Ivoirians, believing that they were different from each other because of ethnic and religious perceptions, no longer had any substantive reason to support corporate or collaborative justice for each other.

As political elites and Ivoirians fought against each other, various developments within different communities had disintegrated, demonstrating some of the crucial challenges in Côte d'Ivoire's national development (Zadi Kessy 2004). Many parts of Côte d'Ivoire were still in need of basic development (Fonds Africain de Developpement 1997).

A Deeper Divide: Coups and Demands

On September 19, 2002, frustration with the Ivoirité program and other deplorable conditions in Côte d'Ivoire eventually drew a response from a group of rebel soldiers led by Guillaume Soro. They launched a coup/attack on Abidjan, Bouake, and Korhogo, a move that clearly declared their vote of no-confidence on President Gbagbo. The coup was not completely successful. The rebels were unable to secure Abidjan because troops loyal to Gbagbo stopped them, but they controlled Bouake and Korhogo. Soro's rebel group finally identified itself as the Mouvement Patriotique de Côte d'Ivoire (MPCI)—Patriotic Movement of Côte d'Ivoire.

At this point the nation was split in two, the North in the hands of the rebels and the South under President Gbagbo's control. The attempted coup had done much damage, causing the deaths of hundreds including General Guéï and his wife. However, because of increased tension, additional rebel groups, namely Mouvement Populaire de Ivorian du Grand Ouest (MPIGO) (Popular Movement of West Ivoirians) and Mouvement Pour la Justice et la Paix (MPJ) (Movement for Justice and Peace), emerged, all asking for roughly the same things: fairness, recognition, and participation. Eventually all the rebel forces joined together to form the Forces Nouvelles (FN)—New Forces (Skogseth 2006).

Between 2002 and 2008, the coup and crisis created difficult conditions with far-reaching implications for Ivoirians. Within the same period, the Ouagadougou Agreement urged Gbagbo to call for elections in Côte d'Ivoire (Bamba and Adou 2008). However, one of the more popular arguments that emerged at this time focused on the rumor that the Ivoirian conflict was created and managed by outsiders (see Wax 2003), possibly by Liberia and Burkina Faso. There were rumors that Soro and his rebel group were supported by Burkina Faso's President Blaise Campaoré. The other rebel groups (MPIGO and MPJ) which merged with Soro's MPCI to form the FN were also rumored to be supported by Charles Taylor of Liberia. Understandably, President Gbagbo was very disturbed by the idea that neighboring presidents were supporting rebel groups against him. Moreover, several groups played around with the idea that North and South Côte d'Ivoire should split into separate nations (see Bailly 2009). Soro and several others opposed this view, insisting that Côte d'Ivoire was one nation, and that its integration was of utmost importance (Wax 2003).

By 2008, citizenship had become a very difficult experience (Ouédraogo & Sall 2008) and the crisis was linked to high political and economic interests (Morel 2006; International Crisis Group 2004), forcing the question as to where Côte d'Ivoire was headed (Ndiaye 2011). Democracy is significant for the development and sustenance of good governance, civil society, and the protection of people. In addition, it engenders collective participation. But the nation was now in the hands of Gbagbo, who spoke so well about democracy, but was now exhibiting autocratic and dictatorial propensities.

Because the national divide and crisis was much deeper, and had reached a point where social and political experiences were disrupted, some creative Ivoirians began focusing on integrative factors such as respect of rights and constructive development (Obou 2009). Some citizens focused on a roundtable gathering held in Grand Bassam in 2005, as an effort to get to a peaceful resolution of the political conflict (Ikome, Zondi, and Konan 2006). Other citizens spoke about hope (Kotoudi 2004; Koulibaly 2004; Koudou 2006), while others insisted that Côte d'Ivoire was moving toward freedom (Koudou 2006). Spiritual and anthropological options invited Ivoirians to return to the humility of acceding to divine control (spirituality) while recognizing the mortality of the human condition equalized by birth, living, and death (anthropology) (Gazoa 2006; Zahiri-Ziki 2006).

Moreover, some citizens focused on the usefulness of democracy, human rights, good governance, and social development (The Centre Ivoirien de Rescherche Économique et Sociale 2008) and the importance of the environment and the need for its legal protection (Adon 2009; Coulibaly 2011). The environmental protection issue in Côte d'Ivoire, as well as in other African nations, is extremely important. The destruction of the environment by internal and external groups disregards national and ecological rules and philosophies in search of easy revenue (mining, waste and toxic dumping, and so on). The problem though is that in the face of national civil strife, environmental concern is the last thing on the minds of the political elite.

What was abundantly rampant was food shortage (Doukoure 2002). If Ivoirians were experiencing a food shortage, then they may have experienced other deprivations. With food poverty comes water poverty, medicine, and healthcare poverty, as well as inadequate housing and other challenges. In addition, the "Survey of Households Living Ivory Coast 2002: Education and Poverty in Côte d'Ivoire" showed the gaps between the upper and lower strata of the Ivoirian society (Okon 2002). The upper echelon did not worry much about survival because they had the means to sustain themselves.

Finally, political power is service and true democracy requires a conception of power as service (Duhy 2006). The expectation for transition to democracy was optimistic but cautious (Goba 2000). Unfortunately, when Gbagbo took office and did not nullify the Ivoirité program set in place by Bédié, the optimism for democracy began to evaporate. The spirit of Bédié's Ivoirité was outrageous and a violation of the cultural and ethnic fusion that came to form Côte d'Ivoire (Gonnin 2006), and Gbagbo and his political machine had come close to assassinating fraternity (Holy 2006). In other words, Ivoirians no longer viewed each other as relatives or kinfolks of the same nation. Instead, they viewed each other as enemies separated by ethnicity. Disengaging citizens from working together around common national identity is destructive and a foundation for social conflict.

Conversely, Ivoirian political elites were instead caught up in subjective political projects that brought them economic benefits (International Crisis Group 2004). This includes enormous embezzlement of funds, fraud for personal benefit, the disregard of human rights and dignity, and summary executions (Dumas and Vergès 2011; Dutheuill 2008; International Crisis Group 2004).

By 2005, Gbagbo had already been in power for about five years, and between 2005 and 2009, several attempts were made by internal groups and the UN to try to get him to call for elections, to no avail. A once-successful Côte d'Ivoire was now being propped up by nongovernmental organizations (NGOs) sustaining some of the basic needs of poor Ivoirians (see Koffi 2008). This downturn was inevitable as monies were drawn out of circulation and used to buy armaments, extensive protection such as paying the Alliance des Jeune Patriotes (AJP) (Young Patriots AJP—mostly Gbagbo loyalists) to prop up the regime, and to fuel personal sustenance requirements.

Closely linked to the foregoing is the corruption of government officials, who in time of national crisis found ways to exploit the poor and embezzle funds through various mismanagement schemes (International Crisis Group 2004). In addition, the crisis led to uncertainty about civility, security, and family cohesion (Koné 2005). Families broke up and had to forage away from each other in order to survive. The coup and the civil war also created casualties, leaving orphans and widows who assumed roles as single parents or guardians to surviving children. In some cases, children became parents overnight as they assumed the care of their siblings. Migration split families apart and completed the massive fragmentation caused by conflict and war.

Despite the invitation offered to Ivoirians to think positively about hope, and to engage the spiritual and reinstate humility and compassion, political elites were too far gone. They had shifted from the spiritual and anthropological to neo-liberal capitalist dimensions of subjective life. The only talk of spirituality was when political elites suggested that God was on their side and guiding them to sit in power indefinitely so as to prevent the devils (political opponents) in the nation from ascending to the presidency and other governance positions. As well, by 2006, Côte d'Ivoire was already too far embroiled in its intractable conflict that only violence and intimidation were the preferred approach to conflict resolution. *Côte d'Ivoire: The Horsemen of the Apocalypse* simply depicts political elite as mad riders riding the nation into the oblivion of interminable misery (Koui 2010).

The last remark in this chapter points to a disturbing fact that from the Ivoirian independence in 1960 to Gbagbo presidency and crisis, women were conspicuously missing as important voices of reason. Nonetheless, there were some Baoulé women who integrated into the Ivoirian political elite grid (Assié-Lumumba 1996). Their way into lower-rung political offices was probably made possible by Houphouët-Boigny and top political elites who were Baoulé. However, they were never allowed into the highest political offices, such as the office of the presidency or prime minister. The few Baoulé and other groups of women given access to elite privileges and low-level governance services does not nullify the social justice concern about the requirement of equal opportunity for women and men to participate in shared political governance.

Chapter Three

Gbagbo and Ouattara Clash

This chapter discusses the specific scenario of the presidential conflict between Gbagbo and Ouattara which occurred between 2010 and 2011. The nature of the conflict was such that the two presidents employed various tactics to destroy each other's chances of holding on to or getting to the presidency. The second section of the chapter explores the implications of governance, power, and social justice.

THE PRESIDENTIAL CONFLICT

There was undoubtedly a power struggle between the two presidents (see, for instance, Attebi 2011; Charvin 2011; Dumas and Vergès 2011; Gakunzi 2011; Ndiaye 2011; Quenum 2011a, 2011b; Toubabou 2011; Agou 2010). The conflict was linked to socio-political activities of the years prior to the presidential conflict (Quenum 2011a; Dumas and Vergès 2011; Agou 2010), and it is also anchored in colonial and post-colonial behavior (Tiabas 2009; Ottemey 2009).

The circumstances surrounding the elections were extremely complex. Gbagbo ran the country for ten years from 2000 to 2010, and refused to relinquish power. Ouattara was declared the winner of the November 28, 2010, elections. Thabo Mbeki (former South African president) insisted that the problem between the two presidents must be resolved with negotiations but submitted a scathing report that appeared to challenge conventional agreement on who won the election (Mbeki 2011). Mbeki's analysis notwithstanding, conventional data insisted that Ouattara had 54.10 percent against 45.90 percent gained by incumbent President Gbagbo. Ouattara's victory was validated and certified by Côte d'Ivoire's Independent Electoral Commission (CEI). Special representatives of the UN secretary (Ban Ki-Moon) in Côte d'Ivoire also validated and certified Ouattara's win (certified by the head of UN operations in Côte d'Ivoire—UNOCI). However and without any warning, the Constitutional Court of Côte d'Ivoire (CCIC) declared Gbagbo the winner with 51 percent of votes. Why the discrepancy between the CEI and UN and the CCIC?

By December 1999, Côte d'Ivoire had moved closer to national civil strife, having been agitated by Bédié's regime because of the changes he made to Houphouët-Boigny's "Open Door Policy" and his institution of Ivoirité. The North, mostly Islamic, and the South, mostly Christian, entered a showdown that led the country to civil strife in the form of a nearly successful coup led by Guillame Soro in 2002. The North was specifically angry because they had been cut off from common rights and privileges in Côte d'Ivoire. Bédié and then Gbagbo were involved in various levels of human rights violations and polarization of the nation, as well as the minimization of social justice options in the country. Bédié, General Guéï, and Gbagbo had brought the nation to a point of inevitable collapse. It is ironic that—in a nation that was so full of promise and a bright example to much of West Africa—a military coup in 1999 ended Bédié's presidency and the influence of the PDCI (a party which originated in 1946 with Houphouët-Boigny—the father of the nation), and a few years later in 2002, another coup almost toppled Gbagbo (Quenum 2011b; Gakunzi 2011).

The two coups could be explained in terms of their differences. The 1999 coup was focused on the general disenchantment in the nation. Ivoirian citizens were involved in demonstrations because of labor, education, lack of wage remuneration, and increasing poor conditions. Citizens had good memories of a recently successful Côte d'Ivoire (1960s to the early 1980s) and were demanding substantive socio-economic and socio-political changes. The leader of the coup, General Guéï, was once the military chief appointed by Houphouët-Boigny in 1990, but was fired by Bédié in 1995 and dismissed from the army in 1997.

In addition to the national agitation, General Guéï, who was of the Yacouba ethnic group from Western Côte d'Ivoire, had some personal grudges against Bédié, and a military coup was the perfect solution. Thus, the 1999 coup was distinctly different from the 2002 almost-successful coup which split the country into two, with the rebels holding on to the North and President Gbagbo and his loyalists holding on to the South. The 2002 coup which came from the North was clearly a response to the anger and frustration with the Ivoirité program and the many abuses that it had institutionalized.

By 2010, the Ivoirian social context was completely divided into hostile polarities, ethnic anger, North and South issues, political intolerance, and fragmented national governance (Gakunzi 2011). Ethnic and identity polarization had been fomented by Bédié through the introduction of the Ivoirité program, but when Gbagbo took office in 2000, instead of dissolving the program, he simply continued to indirectly favor it. For Gbagbo, the advantage of Ivoirité was its use in excluding Ouattara (his political nemesis), most northerners and their possible support of Ouattara, and many others considered half-Ivoirians from participating in the Ivoirian political governance. It is interesting that Gbagbo chose to add to the national polarization even though he ran as a democratic political underdog, all through from Houphouët-Boigny's era until he got into office in 2000.

However, even though the 2002 coup (that almost toppled Gbagbo) drove home the seriousness of the national socio-political conflict, it only forced him to entrench his political views and to hold a more rigid course. That rigidity introduced international leaders (mostly African) into Côte d'Ivoire to help mediate the Ivoirian political impasse. Several agreements followed, namely the Marcoussis Agreement (January 2003), the Accra II Agreement (March 2003), the Accra III Agreement (July 2004), the Pretoria/Tshwane Agreement (April 2005), and finally the Ouagadougou Agreement (March 2007), all of which were tactically disregarded by Gbagbo.

For instance, in the Pretoria/Tshwane Agreement of April 7, 2005, all major conflict parties present (President Laurent Gbagbo, Prime Minister Seydou Diarra, Guillaume Soro—the Northern New Forces Rebel leader, Henri Konan Bédié—former president, Alassane Ouattara—former Prime Minister) pledged to respect all previous agreements, including dismantling rebel militia, demobilizing and integrating Guillaume Soro's northern forces (the FN) into the regular Ivoirian National army, and scheduling presidential elections in October 2005. The conflict parties even requested the United Nations' support in helping to organize, certify, and validate the election (Gakunzi 2011; Quenum 2011b), but the agreement, especially calling for elections, was never fully respected.

However, Gbagbo's consistent behavior and actions in sabotaging the settlement agreements had created a pattern that moved further away from democratic ideals. This pattern would dominate much of his presidency until the elections conflict in 2010. Thus Ivoirians saw the presidential conflict between Gbagbo and Ouattara as a ploy by Gbagbo to stay in office indefinitely (Gakunzi 2011). It was also viewed as an attempt to manipulate the will of Ivoirians (Quenum 2011c, paragraph 26), and Gbagbo was seen as an individual with no moral and ethical compass who set out to dismantle the foundations of justice and fair political governance (Gakunzi 2011).

Other circumstances also contributed to the presidential conflict. What became a deep Ivoirian socio-political problem may in part have its roots in the colonial, political, and geographic arrangement designed by France. The French combined what is now Côte d'Ivoire with what was then Upper Volta (now the nation of Burkina Faso) as one large French territory. This arrangement lasted until the 1940s (Amondji 1986) when Upper Volta was separated into its own territory and later gained independence as a sovereign nation (later renamed itself as Burkina Faso).

It is impossible to imagine that those who chose to stay in Burkina Faso and those who chose to stay in Côte d'Ivoire were are not linked psycho-socially, geographically, culturally, and in other ways. The populations were forever linked together through intermarriage, work, and regional/national identity. Bédié, using neo-colonial as well as personal vindictive logic, exploited the vulnerability of the intricate interaction by imposing Ivoirité to segregate, marginalize, and violate human rights (see Ndlovu-Gatsheni 2010).

This, of course, raises the question of deservingness and undeservingness in Côte d'Ivoire (see Langer 2005). It usually takes ideologies of hate and ethnocentrism to negatively stir up antagonism in any social context. When advantageous, the rich and poor, or Muslims and Christians, or different ethnic groups use the ideologies to create negation, alienation, marginalization, and even violence. Consider that by 2010, the conflict groups in Côte d'Ivoire utterly despised each other. The hate and negating ideologies were powerful enough that each group could manipulate allegiance in view of constructing social divisiveness and social injustices. This was certainly the case in Rwanda, Nazi Germany, Cambodia, and Bosnia. In Côte d'Ivoire, as in most volatile conflict scenarios, the multifaceted social damages were orchestrated by the political elite.

It took some pressure from the UN and other international groups to get Gbagbo to finally agree to conduct elections in October 2010 (Gakanzi 2011; Quenum 2011b). However, Gbagbo's unwillingness to let go of power and his nullification of votes from nine regions of the country led him to get the CCIC to manipulate the constitution, citing article 94 to certify his win with 51 percent of votes so that he could continue as president. This was clearly a contradiction of the CEI's conclusion which supplied a 54.10 percent win for Ouattara against 45.90 percent for Gbagbo. The CCIC could not usurp power and arbitrarily proclaim Gbagbo as president because in the Pretoria agreement of April 7, 2005, all sides agreed that an independent monitor and a certifier of the election (the CEI) should serve as convener and arbiter for the elections (Quenum 2011b). The CCIC, an already untrustworthy legal machine (Quenum 2011b), capitulated to Gbagbo and overstepped its legal parameters.

As the conflict protracted, Gbagbo drummed up support and manipulated sentiments against the northerners whom he claimed were foreign immigrants from Burkina Faso. He also insisted that Ouattara was a half-Ivoirian northerner who was in bed with international power systems, the IMF, and the World Bank. As far as he was concerned, cutting Ouattara off would be beneficial to his regime. In addition, Gbagbo drummed up nationalism against the UN and other international bodies which he claimed were interfering in a domestic dispute (Gakunzi 2011; Quenum 2011c).

This form of nationalism, especially one that conjures up all kinds of colonial, neo-colonial, and imperialistic cabalism cooked up in foreign places to outwit Africans, has always been used in many African nations as a way to foment internal support (i.e., in South Africa during apartheid, and the Mugabe scenario in Zimbabwe). Naturally, Gbagbo's perception was that whatever the international community was recommending in terms of asking him to respect the elections results could not be good for the country because they were the ones who got Africa and specifically Côte d'Ivoire to its present conditions in the first place.

The conflict between the two presidents was a nightmare. Ivoirians saw the first independence as wresting Côte d'Ivoire from France, and now the second independence was to wrestle it from tyranny (Charvin 2011), dictatorship, and mediocrity created not by foreign systems but by Ivoirian political elites struggling to hold on to political power. To that effect, Gbagbo was asked to step down by the CEI, the UN, ECOWAS, the AU, the EU, France, and the United States among several nations that certified the elections results. Gbagbo was clearly in the wrong but continued to claim that improprieties in the elections led to Ouattara's November 28, 2010, win.

For instance, Gbagbo had difficulty accepting Youssouf Bakayoko's (the chairman of the CEI) announcement, which he claimed was made without CEI members at the Goff Hotel which served as Ouattara's elections headquarters. As response, Gbagbo ordered votes from nine regions of the country annulled (Ivory Coast Poll Overturned 2010). In other words, Gbagbo insinuated with this action that Bakayoko and Ouattara manipulated the numbers to Ouattara's favor. Bakayoko's part in the conflict was captured by news reports. News showed intimidation of Bakayoko and members of the CEI when they were overseeing the elections. In fear for his life, Bakayako escaped (slipped out unannounced) to the Goff Hotel for refuge, and subsequently made the announcement of the elections results there (Oved 2010).

Moreover, Gbagbo adopted an inflexible stance because the first round of the elections (though not technically useful for a win) declared him the winner with 38.04 percent and Ouattara with 32.07 percent. It was in the second round that the tables turned and Ouattara had 54.1 percent and Gbagbo had 45.9 percent (Le Patriote 2011; Ivory Coast Poll Overturned 2010; Oved 2010). Basing his argument on his success in the first round of election, assuming that Ouattara and his supporters somehow rigged the election, and insisting that Ouattara's win was an "attempted coup" (Oved 2010), he decided that staying put was the best option. It is not clear what Gbagbo was thinking, but one speculation is that he strongly believed that the standoff would lead to an internal struggle which his loyal troops and militia would eventually resolve with violence. In other words, Gbagbo knew he lost but insisted that Ouattara's win in the second run-off was a fluke.

After a fact-finding mission to Côte d'Ivoire, former South African president Thabo Mbeki, who himself was leader of a nation that had recently resolved one of the world's most hideous racist legacies, submitted to the AU that negotiation was the best way to resolve the conflict between the two presidents. His reasons were simple. The conditions and circumstances in Côte d'Ivoire and the conflict were so complex that any other option would lead to civil strife and untold misery on vulnerable citizens (Thabo Mbeki Begins 2010). His view was contrary to a unanimous world opinion which recognized Ouattara as the winner and demanded that Gbagbo step down.

Gbagbo's insistence on holding on to power caused an adverse reaction from the international community. The African Union (AU), the Economic Community of West Africa (ECOWAS), the European Union (EU), the United States, and other international bodies simply cut diplomatic ties with Gbagbo's government. His ministers were on the no-fly list of the United States and the EU, making his elite governing group persona non grata to their favorite recreational places in the Western world. Conversely, Ouattara used his extensive international network to call on the IMF, the World Bank, and the BCEAO, as well as the Africa Development Bank (ADB) to stop doing business with Gbagbo.

In April of 2011, the northern army now under Ouattara's control fought their way to the South, surrounded Gbagbo at the Presidential Palace in Abidjan, and with the help of the UN and French forces, arrested him, clearing the way for Ouattara to be finally enthroned as the president of Côte d'Ivoire (Gakanzi 2011; Ndiaye 2011; Quenum 2011d; Toubabou 2011). With Gbagbo's arrest, the conflict between the presidents was over. However, because of deep fragmentation, especially in terms of the absence of good governance, low positive political will, and absence of social justice, post-conflict challenges would require collaborative and transformative efforts to bring about and sustain a working civil society in a democratic context.

Uses of Governance, Power, and Social Justice

In some cases, judicial review of government action in terms of administrative justice, legal doctrine, and legal procedures has been useful, but in other cases not (Forsyth et al. 2010). Because much of the time, governance systems structure around unequal representation, a popular and strong movement toward de-politicization of public issues and interests may be useful for better governance. Furthermore, the way in which socio-political arrangements center around elitist institutional structures deliberately disorients public participation (Törnquist, Webster, and Stokke 2009). This was the case in Côte d'Ivoire for much of its conflict history. Elite politicians simply constructed the governance system to their advantage and fought over who among them should sit on top of the food chain.

For this reason, there ought to be decentralization of issues, and better and more robust interaction between government and society (see Tendler 1998). It is interesting that the World Bank captures the concerns and aspirations of those seeking the decentralization of local and metropolitan governance activities. In places where decentralized government exists, there seems to be some hope for progress more than in those places where they don't exist (World Bank 2009).

The nature of power has been intensely debated for centuries. Power is configured in so many ways, but in terms of its use in governance, it appears more structured on the superior-subordinate dynamic than anything else. The Ivoirian situation was the exact replication of the excesses of power openly displayed as a form of punishment described by Foucault in his 1975 *Discipline and Punish* (1977). From Foucault's assessment, it may be concluded that Ivoirians were trapped prisoners being punished by their political elites. The only difference from the scenario that Foucault described in his piece is that Ivoirians are citizens of a nation under a wave of brutal hegemonic rage.

Others such as Greene (2000) take the more frightening approach by encouraging people not to avoid taking up and using power because it is part of the human reality. He organizes power into forty-eight laws, and his advice to readers to excel in using power so as not to become powerless may have served as an excellent handbook for the Ivoirian political elites. Since power by itself is applicable to how human beings interact with each other (some dominant and others less dominant), when it is attached to political activities, a form of manic control emerges that is inflexible as much as it is draconian. Perhaps Greene's point that it is better to excel in taking up and using power to one's advantage rather than assume powerlessness helps explain why the Ivoirian elite cultivated their political power dynamics in ways that portrayed them as indomitable and inflexible.

However, beyond the question of power and its implication, there is also concern about social justice. Part of the struggle for fairness during the presidential conflict in Côte d'Ivoire was hinged on the people's desire for a civil distributive justice system. A focus on social justice in any nation cannot occur unless the government and its citizens collaborate on establishing options for civil society and good governance. Since everyone does not have the same talents, are not the same age, and do not have equal experiences, adopting Sen's (1992, 1999, 2001) common values such as freedom and individual capabilities may be a useful way to reorganize popular notions about inequality, freedom, and self-determination. The concern about the approach of empowering individual capability not easily measureable or enacted into public policy is muted by the preponderance of its utility in terms of linking it to the resolution of poverty and justice issues (Comim, Qizilbash, and Alkire 2008).

So in Côte d'Ivoire, the extensive socio-economic concerns where Ivoirians found themselves without jobs and salaries, and saddled with inequalities and other social difficulties, demonstrated that the traditional approach of touting economic recovery and social quick fixes was not going to be enough. Resources and tools should be made available by the government and private enterprises so that individuals can further their self-determination while simultaneously contributing to social and economic progress. Had several of the political elite been really interested in connecting with their citizens, adopting Sen's common values such as freedom and individual capabilities may have contributed in some ways to the resolution of at least some of the socio-economic impasse.

Unfortunately for Côte d'Ivoire, the monetary resources which ought to have been used for individual capabilities development were used to control civil strife (weapons and self-protection details), as well as embezzled for future personal use (International Crisis Group, 2004).

To sum up this chapter, Sen's (2009) expanded views on his previous thought on capabilities and freedom offer that the usefulness of a decentralized quest for justice and distributive justice opens up the space to rethink social justice in ways that better respond to contemporary conditions. Similarly, the notion of creating capabilities through reexamining human development (Nussbaum 2011), and the consciousness about sustaining the disadvantaged in a distributive grid (Rawls 1971, 2001) pushes the limits on getting people to understand the fundamental nature of justice as something that is essential for social coherence and cohesion.

In additional, Sandel's (2009) popular question for thinking about justice ("what is the right thing to do?") adds to the challenge that doing justice is a collaborative or communitarian affair. Thus, in the case of Côte d'Ivoire, the initial broad-based implication of the presidential conflict was the overt disconnection between government and citizens. Clearly, Côte d'Ivoire's political elite left much to be desired when they were entrusted with governance, political power, and citizens' lives. Response to social injustices, calls for elections, calls for fairness, and the reorganization of social conditions through responsible service to all citizens fell well short of the demands for civil society and democratic considerations.

Chapter Four

The Presidential Conflict through Theoretical Frameworks

The conflict between Presidents Gbagbo and Ouattara in Côte d'Ivoire emerged from an intensely complex socio-political and socio-economic interplay with local and global implications. Six theories (and several others may have been useful as well) helped with nuanced exploration of the conflict.

THE CONFLICT THROUGH ELITE THEORY

For the Ivoirian scenario, the elite theory comes in handy as the conflict was examined from the specific angle that it occurred in a highly stratified social context. The elite theory came from C. Wright Mills (1956) and focuses on power relationships in modern society. Mills explained that a small minority, concretized as economic, political, and policy elite, control all power dynamics. The epistemological framework for this approach is that a concrete divide exists between those who have and use power, and the rest of the population who are mostly at their mercy. The other useful element of this theory is that all economic and political systems are determined and organized to the advantage of the elites.

In Côte d'Ivoire, citizens actually experienced the impact of elite social arrangements. Many Ivoirians were systematically dehumanized, with women relegated to the very bottom of the society. Mills's (1956) critical analysis of the structure of society led to one encompassing conclusion, that the "Power Elite" broken into three substantive groups (political, economic, and military)—and this is true in Côte d'Ivoire—had total control of power dynamics.

Thus, Mills's *White Collar* (1951) and *The Power Elite* (1956) were focused on the perspective that society was always organized to the advantage of a few people having total power over others. To counteract this arrangement, he offered that arming the public with information about the nature of power distribution in society is helpful in creating an important social shift that may profoundly change class and other social configurations. For the Côte d'Ivoire scenario, it was clear that the elite controlled everything. Unfortunately, Mills's notion of arming people with the required information useful for transformation was not possible in Côte d'Ivoire because of the massive disjunction there.

Moreover, this kind of transformation arrangement is not possible in Côte d'Ivoire because political elites believe that they are the only ones who can generate and sustain society with their ideas and philosophies. They also have a tremendous advantage over the rest of the population because there is still a large segment of Ivoirians with no access to crucial information useful for dealing with making decisions and choices about economic, social, religious, and political issues. Ivoirian political elites also continue to insist that without their leadership, "irrational Ivoirians" (or the riff raff) will lead Côte d'Ivoire to economic, political, and social collapse.

By Gbagbo's presidency, Ivoirian political elites were insisting that the solution to the Ivoirian socio-political conflict is not shared governance, shared political power, or the accession to a civil society wherein presidential and other political office term limits are respected. Ivoirian elites' narrative insisted that its control of governance and political power is always the best option. To sustain this narrative, the Ivoirian political elite appeared anchored on the notion that Côte d'Ivoire was economically, politically, and socially successful under Houphouët-Boigny (an elite autocratic dictator) who tightly controlled everything.

Not surprisingly, most political elites would argue that mass participation in political activities, beyond just being citizens and voting (often rigged) is detrimental to the overall image of the political system. They would also insist that the decentering approaches brought about by coups, rebel activities, and multi-party meddling ruined Côte d'Ivoire. For the elites then, the presidential conflict is not actually the problem of the two presidents, but the result of the irrationality of some members with anarchistic notions urging the masses to engage in civil strife and conditions with unpredictable and dangerous consequences. Of course, within the elite theoretical context only political elites are right and can fix the mess that has occurred in Côte d'Ivoire.

Moyo (2009) appears to support dictatorial elitism as she argues that before democracy and civil society can really take shape in many African nations, they need powerful dictator-like leaders who would whip things into shape. Giving her some benefit of doubt, Moyo probably means positive and citizen-centered dictator leaders, but her position clearly sustained President Gbagbo's elitism. Gbagbo, viewing himself as more knowledgeable and more politically savvy than all Ivoirians, entrenched his stubborn insistence on dictatorial autocracy. He clamped down on all liberatory agitations and negated several efforts to entertain negotiations in view of anchoring democracy and civil society in Côte d'Ivoire.

The Conflict through Neo-Marxist Conflict Theory

From a different angle, neo-Marxist conflict theory suggests that society is froth with concrete disagreements based on conflicts between dominant and disadvantaged groups. The two feuding presidents were from two distinct ethnic groups, which were totally opposed to each other. Neo-Marxists insist that conflicts, therefore, are the result of social arrangements, many of which guarantee benefits to dominant members and disadvantages to others (Vanoutrivel 1977). Rawls (1971), for example, delineated that justice and fairness are a function of equal opportunities in terms of access to the distribution of life-sustaining common resources. This access includes political power and economic opportunities, shared governance, and the benefits of a civil society. Unfortunately, dominant members of societies manipulate social arrangements to favor unequal distribution which dispossesses already disadvantaged populations.

Dahrendorf (1959), a key proponent of contemporary conflict theory, points out that the world is not quite static as formalized by functionalism, but is always in flux because of the presence and interacting dynamics of conflict. Considering the presidential conflict from this angle, one explanation may be that the Ivoirian power elites' effort to corral all Ivoirians into a submissive lot under autocratic dictatorship neglected the reality that such a move would generate massive conflict between groups. In other words, the presidential conflict is an indication of the disconnection and isolation of political elites from the rest of the population. Another explanation may be that the Ivoirian political elite did not anticipate that those they had dismissed as docile and naïve citizens, exploitable with negative governance and political power, were capable of sustaining their quest for democracy and civil society.

Exploiting many citizens as docile and ignorant subordinates, exploiting their labor internally (menial jobs, cocoa and coffee farm labor, etc.), and not offering many of them democratic access, self-determination, and distributive justice was a recipe for conflict.

Neo-Marxist conflict theorists would view elites of any society as select members of the dominant group who construct realities as they see fit. This group socially constructs perspectives to strip ordinary citizens of their rights, privileges, and dignity. Thorstein Veblen (1908), in his *Leisure Class*, clarified how elites as a group emerged. This group viewed labor as beneath them, and so an interesting way of life emerged which required no manual labor, but which deified intellectual or other such activities as more useful in creating and managing the elements and systems that lay the foundation of society.

In addition, elites generally view those they view as inferior (most citizens) as daft and dangerous to social order. Elites also consider their "status" and "rational" moves as better suited for the construction of national, political, economic, social, geographic, environmental, and even global policies. This is why political elites insist that only certain top rational individuals should be at the helm of socio-political and socio-economic systems.

Conversely, the neo-Marxist conflict theorist would expose political elites as individuals who are generally unwilling to blame themselves as the architects of bad governance and political doom, such as occurred in Côte d'Ivoire. For Côte d'Ivoire, neo-Marxists would point out that society could be a better place when access and collaborative experience evolve into genuine democracy and civil society flourishes.

The Conflict through Rational Choice Theory

Ritzer and Goodman (2004) point to something quite intriguing when they examined the philosophy of intentionality in rational choice theory. When actions occur, actors point these actions toward some goal. This is to suppose that rational choice theory views actors and actresses engaged in transactions as involved in some sort of a rational activity. This activity is intentioned on goals drawn to have significance in terms of the agreements of participants. Thus, in the case of the Ivoirian presidential conflict, this theory would assume that all Ivoirians are rational and that engaging each other was carefully reasoned out in terms of the acquiescence to a political system and the use of leaders to run it.

For rational choice proponents, society in conflict is not always the formula for consistent contractual interaction. In fact, conflict is less the issue than a mutual focus on some goal. So that for political leaders and citizens, the mutual goal is to get their lives from one point to another, whatever that other point is determined to be by majority of the citizens. The choices presented by the national leaders and the political system, and the rational choice of the citizens to freely choose representatives in the hope of creating a sense of well-being, fall under the rational prescription, nullifying the sense of perpetual conflict postulated by neo-Marxist conflict theory.

Thus, the focus is on rational relationships exemplified by mutual contracts. From this perspective, the presidential conflict in Côte d'Ivoire occurred within the conditions of well-thought-out rational activities rather than as conflicts between competing individuals/groups. What the rational choice theorists do not take into consideration is the dangers embedded in the hidden agenda of political elites which are incomprehensible to the most astute rational citizens. When the poor and disadvantaged citizens are factored into the process, the philosophy of rational choice collapses. The other real question is the one identified by MacIntyre (1981, 1988) which clarified that contemporary rationality was actually a new form of manipulation, namely emotivism. This raises the question as to whether conditions in Côte d'Ivoire before and during the presidential conflict were organized around rational or subjective and dangerous emotive postulations.

The Conflict through Intergroup Conflict Theory

Intergroup conflict theory understands that conflict occurs between different groups because of differences such as ethnicity, race, class, educational level, gender, sexual orientation, and so on. In this case, group identity and categorical social and geographic space signification drive conflict. Allport (1954), Doise (1978), and Tajfel and Turner (1979) all helped in capturing the dynamics of group conflict either through seeking to understand, for instance, the nature of prejudices (Allport 1954), or seeking to understand the nature of social identification with a group (Tajfel and Turner 1979). The idea of intergroup conflict is that it feeds on constructing categorizations and differentiation (Folger, Poole, and Stutman 2005).

Despite its ethnic and religious diversity (see Simons and Fennig's 2017 ethnologue.com; Skogseth 2006), Côte d'Ivoire—an all-African nation—still had conditions that generated conflict. When Bédié instituted the Ivoirité doctrine (pure Ivoirian = born of two Ivoirian parents) in 1995 during his tenure as Ivoirian president (from 1993–1999), he most probably excited the negative differences in the ethnic and religious identities of Ivoirians. He understood that communicating any sentiment of social differentiation would create a rigid caste system which would tactically cut off northern Ivoirians from all access to common national resources. The forcing of Ivoirité into national consciousness and its manipulation and use by most southerners set off the larger conflict that lingered in Côte d'Ivoire for about two decades, and eventually culminated in the specific conflict between Presidents Gbagbo and Ouattara.

In Côte d'Ivoire, the nature of ethnicity is such that dominant ethnic groups view their identity as being members of a significant, dominant, and deserving group. This view, of course, discounts or minimizes other ethnic groups' significance. For instance, while Bédié was president of Côte d'Ivoire, he argued that the Boaulé and Agni ethnic groups were the only ones with political leadership capabilities (Skogseth 2006). This kind of polarization ideologically discounted some ethnic groups and their capabilities and created unnecessary polarizing conflict. During the conflict, less dominant ethnic and religious groups were forced to insert themselves into political, economic, and social participation in order to survive. The national conflict that ensued in Côte d'Ivoire eventually led to the presidential conflict because groups (the elite, ostracized northerners, powerful political parties and opponents, polarized ethnic groups, and agitated poor Ivoirians) were all struggling for political power, rights, privileges, and/or access to common national resources.

The Conflict through Postmodern Theory

Postmodern social theorists (Foucault 2002; Guattari 1995; Lyotard 1979; Baudrillard 1979; Deleuze and Guattari 1972) and many others are dissatisfied with the configurations of the modernist agenda. Smart (1993) shows three dimensions of how people came to view postmodernism: those who seek a complete break from modernity called the new era the postmodern era (see Baudrillard 1979; Deleuze 1972; Guattari 1995), those who see elements of the modern still present in the postmodern (Jameson 1991; Nicholson 1999), and then those who claim that postmodern theory is an epistemological exercise that critiques everything in modernity (Smart falls under this group).

What is important, though, is that no matter the version of postmodern theory, its theorists view their efforts as responding to the different excesses of modernity. For instance, even though postmodernism charges full force against liberal and humanistic configurations of modernity, some scholars using postmodernist theory (critical race, gay/lesbian, social displacement, and so on) have drawn the analysis to much deeper nuances, insisting that the miseries of modernity juxtaposed with the search for liberation justify a postmodernist approach. The idea then according to Smart (1993) is to expose the modernist content by way of critiquing it. A useful summary then would be that modernity is a sham, a place where static functionalism was encouraged, and the subterfuges to dupe and dehumanize people were concretized.

For the postmodern social theorist, modernity is characterized by wars, abuse, genocide, destruction of disadvantaged populations, and capitalist schemes that take advantage of people's sense of reality and freedom. In addition, academics, politicians, and bureaucrats in modernity arbitrarily impose their picayune worldviews on everyone as if that was all that mattered. The postmodern social theorist explains social aberrations as a modernist catastrophe based on modern significations. In modernity, the virtual is made real (Las Vegas, Disneyland, etc.) and "real" reality is fragmented into useless and meaningless simulacra. Signs that modernity is a sham are everywhere: the death of marriage, revolutions, wars, genocide, the end of freedom, the pathologies of the mass population who after being abused are dumped into mass misery, vacuous shopping malls, asylums (Foucault's depiction), and mass physical and mental prisons.

In modernity, incarceration, brutal police and court actions, and capitalism all compound to abuse humanity in unimaginable ways. For the postmodern social theorist, the actual criminals are the modern bureaucrats, economists, and politicians. For postmodern theory, all social modernist arrangements are deconstructable and should be exposed as shams, concocted by irrational and inebriated maniacs wielding extremist and negative power to control human beings and social contexts. There was never any specific destiny for anyone, let alone one that is designed by power-hungry maniacs insisting that they have answers to social problems. No one has answers to anything. Everyone's view is equal and is useful for achieving or doing anything. Postmodern social theory disconnects people from the safety nets they crave, and exposes the emptiness of modernist fabrications of coherent social arrangements.

Postmodern theory would explain the Ivoirian presidential conflict and the national crises that led to it in several ways. First, it would argue that the nature of social arrangements in Côte d'Ivoire has generally been beneficial to a specific group of people (the elite and the powerful who also own the means of production and control political power). To the modernist Ivoirian elite and power brokers, society is like a predetermined game, and they alone can influence who wins or loses. Depending on how they feel, they construct ethnic differentiation (Bédié), ethnic conflict, and civil strife; cut off entire segments of Ivoirians from access to resources; displace the Muslim religious group; and superimpose an autocratic dictatorial homogeneity and hegemony on the nation.

From this angle, the Ivoirian conflict is a signification of total collapse in the confidence of the ruling elite and their refusal to accept the simplest positive inventions of the modern eras namely, democracy and civil society. From another angle, postmodernists may posit that there are two eras in Côte d'Ivoire, the modern and the postmodern. For the powerful political elite whose epistemological paraphernalia are Western education configured to maximize pleasure and comfort in the Ivoirian social context, the modern era has ended and the postmodern era is driving their agenda. The elite and powerful forces in Côte d'Ivoire who benefited tremendously from the modernist agenda are now in the postmodern era, but still want to use modern-era laws to subjugate massive numbers of people in the modern era. There is an advantage to this tactic. It is convenient and much easier to manipulate people in the modern era into obsequiousness and docility. Because social experience in the postmodern era is far more eclectic, subversive, and extremely individualistic, the Ivoirian elite and power brokers try to block access to this era because of the fear of losing control of privileges and power.

Refusing to allow people access into the postmodern era has consequences. Since Ivoirians have been struggling for a long time to free themselves from the chains of the modern era (colonization, imperialism, neocolonization, and so on), their awareness that democracy is preferable over dictatorship and their refusal to continue settling for the modernist agenda of massive exploitation translates into conflict with the ruling elite. The specific conflict between the presidents may be explained in terms of both presidents seeking to assert their distinctive deconstructive perspective as to what would be useful to Côte d'Ivoire. The postmodern theorist would simply argue that the larger Ivoirian conflict, which culminated in the specific presidential conflict, was inevitable and will continue to recur over and over until a shift to a new form of governance which allows participation in a decentered civil society occurs. This would be a place and space where Ivoirians would be able to fully explore their individual self-determinations, coalescing into uncomfortable but reconstructed social experiences.

However, some theorists are uncomfortable with any version of postmodernism. For instance, the functionalist stratification theory popularized by David and Moore (1945) focuses on the nature of social stratification. The general idea of the theory is that every society has a form of socially stratified population with assigned social positions. These functionalist stratification theorists insist that society is organized around the positions and the rules that govern them. These rules, in turn, are configured in such a way that everyone is remunerated based on whether they have high or low participation. However, these positions are linked to the roles people play to keep society functional and moving forward.

Moreover, these positions and roles are also useful and important for structural stability. Generally, functionalism views the world as a place where order rather than chaos is the determining force for social integration. For this reason, functionalist stratification theory would view the postmodernist theoretical explanation of the Ivoirian presidential conflict as missing the point. In fact, as far as the functionalists in their varieties are concerned, postmodernist theory causes more disintegration, adding to the social disarray wrought by deliberately swaying from the tenets of functional stratification. To the functionalist stratification theorists, the Ivoirian presidential conflict occurred because social political elites failed to stay in their positions, respect the rule of law, and perform assigned roles of service to the nation.

As well, they would argue that instead of sustaining the society through position/role performances in stratified contexts, the two powerful presidents, as well as people who had no business in political governance, indulged in behaviors and actions that were antithetical to social order and cohesion. The presidential conflict is naturally the consequence of this belligerence. In other words, functionalist stratification theory would blame people for indulging in unassigned behaviors. Their logic would be that when people move about without clearly assigned positions and roles for which they are talented (who assigns or should assign these roles?—the elite and the powerful?), then things usually get out of hand. What functionalist stratification theorists fail to see is that society never had assigned "natural" positions and roles and that most people were simply coerced into social classes and defined positions. Postmodernism is just a response to and an articulation of the negation of such coercion, specifically in the case of Côte d'Ivoire.

The Conflict through Critical Feminism

Encouraged by race liberation theories (for instance, Cone 1970; Carmichael and Hamilton 1967; and Gutiérrez 1973) which emerged in the 1960s challenging the nature of social arrangement, laws, and systemic social oppression, contemporary women found that hyper-intellectualism was necessary to augment the critique of masculine and patriarchal dominance. By the 1970s and 1980s, a more critical approach to theoretical analysis emerged, flowing easily from the critique of the dehumanization of women to the direct challenge of status quos that bound women in the bondage of a few choices, ineptitude, economic servitude, and submissiveness. By the 1980s Carol Gilligan devised a different voice in terms of how women evaluated the social experiences of women which men took for granted.

The woman's voice was for all purposes distinct from the masculine as Gilligan (1982) demonstrated in her work about how young women think about moral and social challenges. There was a remarkable pattern of caring and collaboration in the feminine experience. Rosemary Radford Ruether (1983), Elizabeth Fiozena (1983), and several others followed with a series of critiques of patriarchy, and in no time critical feminist theory emerged as a counterpunch to the soft feminism that was being critiqued by a diverse group of scholars from around the globe as being Eurocentric and an unconscious adoption of Eurocentric masculine frameworks. There was a need to respond to masculine perspectives not only because women's conditions were subsumed under masculinity, but also because it was necessary to institute appropriate gender relations in general. For this purpose, critical feminist theory came in handy as a tool to dissect social, political, economic, and even common everyday assumptions about women.

In a way, critical feminist theory was about emancipation from masculine socially constructed gender roles. It was also a theoretical process that forced scholars and audiences to examine epistemologies in ways that drove out constrictive ideologies while introducing divergent egalitarian and humanizing discourses and perspectives. Just as critical race theory helped to tease out and challenge those assumptions that were often precluded from public discourse (but were equally pernicious in terms of minimizing distributive justice), critical feminist theory viewed socially constructed dynamics such as inequality, faces of oppression delineated by Young (1990), and legal dynamics, as well as economic, governance, and public policy to be important elements of contestation.

The fundamental usefulness of the theory would be liberatory in the sense that socially constructed values are given their proper subjective characterizations by being dethroned from their previously and coercively ascribed objectivity. The other usefulness of the theory may be found in its articulation of new frameworks, or if you will, new paradigmatic postures that suggest egalitarian collaboration as defining continuity in negotiating all conditions. Thus, critical feminist theory validates the nature of critical theoretical shifts which encourage social integration through consistent interactive reflection that moves from the subjective to the other and back to the subjective in an interminable loop. It is this audacious insight of the critical feminist to examine the self and others in much deeper ways, drawing together the angst of social constraints defined into daily life and enforced by dichotomies and contradictions, that makes critical feminist theory a very useful epistemological tool for analyzing political, economic, and social issues.

Much like critical race theories or queer theories, critical feminist theory uses history and the import of political, economic, and social arrangements to engage the status quo in view of eliciting critical discourses that lead to substantive social change. This approach is also significant if researchers and scholars are to be properly positioned in their ability to link the sources of conflict to the context where people, especially women, suffer the burdens which emerge as consequences. This agrees with Horkheimer's (1972) delineation of critical theory, which seeks to explicate conditions, capture concrete experiences in ways that can be patterned into practice, and wrap up with what should be done as corrective.

The second element comes from the challenge made possible by the rigorous discourse of critical feminist theory itself, which enlivens and enlightens participants by propelling them in various directions in search of alternative and responsible ways of conceptualizing egalitarian and less unequal interactions. Sentiments of this discourse are even found in masculine writings such as Paulo Freire's *Pedagogy of the Oppressed* (1990). This means that it is not just because critical feminist theory is attractive in and of itself because it is drawn and formulated from the experience of those who are oppressed by masculine arrangements; it also welcomes all levels of critical scholarly participation (McCann and Seung-Kyung 2010), some sensitive, some radical (calling for structural changes that would be beneficial at all levels to everyone), and all focused on the third element which purposively pursues social integration in view of properly contextualizing women's experiences and perspectives.

It follows then that using the theory to try to understand the Ivoirian presidential conflict would run along the lines of masculine miscalculations about the implication of political behaviors and social arrangements. Such a behavior which has traditionally excluded women only serves to increase the misery suffered by women in Côte d'Ivoire. Clearly then, when women do not have the same number of spaces at the tables where political decisions and public policies are made, the inevitable consequences of such decisions and their collapse are only too evident. Conversely, critical feminist theorists would argue that the conflict between the two masculine presidents is a symptom of a much deeper social problem where men posit themselves as immutable and fight without regard to the misery unleashed on those beneath them. They would view such a conflict not as one that has integrative merit in the sense that the two presidents are fighting to ensure that a democracy exists where women and men participate equally in governance, but are focused on their masculinity and sustenance of a vacuous subjectivity and violent patriarchy. In addition, they may also explain the conflict in terms of gender population dynamics. The glaring absence of women in political governance arrangements in a nation where women are equal to or more than the population of men can only be explained by the ongoing patriarchal dynasty that refuses to even recognize that women exist and are capable of service to and participation in shared governance.

Somehow, in response to critical feminist theory and its use to explain the Ivoirian presidential conflict, the structural functionalists would add that order, roles, and positions are indispensable for social cohesion. However, their concern about order and roles is less significant in a nation where such order and roles are constructed to have adverse consequences on women. A more useful response comes from the growing collection of literary discourses now commonly called developing world theories. They appear to be a direct response to the quest to contextualize thoughts of feminine writers outside the Western world, as well as their desire to link with and be represented in the larger critical feminist effort.

These collections of theories are mostly a response to developmental issues in their specific regional contexts (Charrad 2001; Sen and Grown 1987). Some of these perspectives expand upon the notion that the various versions of critical feminist theory on gender, structural, and other oppressions often focus on the concerns of core nations. In other words, the context of critical discourses is formalized around Western European experience. This means that when Western feminist theorists try to explain the Ivoirian presidential conflict, there may not be that much of an affinity because of the existing disconnection and distrust between Western and developing nations.

Whereas women in the Western world enjoy nuanced privileges, most women in Côte d'Ivoire are berated, excluded from political power, marginalized, and are often the first to be discarded in all socio-economic and socio-political arrangements. Developing world theories, an articulation of critical feminist theory, would view the Ivoirian presidential conflict as a conflict of position-assertion between insatiable spoiled brats fighting not over how to serve/protect the nation, but over who should have total control of the nation. Such a control guarantees control of national revenue, a source of personal enrichment at the expense of citizens, specifically women.

The Conflict through Internal Corruptive Theory

To enhance the foregoing theories, a theoretical discourse that does not actu ally have a name has been included as a useful evaluative tool. For convenience, I have named it here the "Internal Corruptive Theory." The content of the theory has been written about by many African and Africanist scholars, and it is surprising that there is no direct nomenclature that depicts it in the literature.

In many African nations, the struggle continues to be the search for social, economic, and political stability (Nhema 2004). Since the independence of several African nations from European colonists, indigenous political elites have imposed shortsighted policies on their nations. These policies turn off hope for self-sustaining developmental dynamics. Adedeji (1999) shows that in the forty-eight contiguous Sub-Saharan nations, there were about eighty violent government changeovers between the 1960s and the 1990s. These changes define rampant socio-economic conditions such as poverty and massive health issues (HIV/AIDS, malaria, and much more). Some of these concerns led Jeffrey Sachs (2005) to conclude that the kind of poverty found in many nations of Africa is fatal and terminal.

Nhema (2004) points to some of the crucial elements that militate against social fluidity on the continent and helps make some initial sense of the challenges. These nations have governance problems, which in turn affect their socio-economic and political arrangements, which in turn result in a leadership vacuum. This vacuum stifles civil society wherein the prospect of a thriving democracy helps to sustain a necessary and collaborative social justice dynamic. Nhema's point is that these important elements have not quite taken root. So in these nations, Côte d'Ivoire included, social conflict is rampant and the sources of these conflicts can be traced to governance issues, to social arrangements that benefit the elite, and to the continued mass impoverishment of nations by internal and external policies (Nhema 2004, 12–21).

Somehow government entities in several nations in Africa assume that the matrix of political and social governance is conditioned on the elite theory, insisting that Africans are still traditional, are not ready for complex social systems found in other parts of the world, and are always in need of direction and leadership from dictatorial henchmen. In industrialized and highly technological nations such as the United States, governance, though not in its perfect form, takes the shape of "democratic" collaboration, ensuring that constituents are represented in some way. This process (though imperfect) ensures social, political, and economic sustainability, while also securing some liberties for citizens. This was supposed to be the direction followed by many African nations when they fought for their independence. But since the 1960s the scenarios in Africa have been more defined by conflict (Zewani's 1999 speech to the United Nations cited in Nhema 2004) than anything else.

It is especially troubling to see a clear division in global arrangements and conditions. In some parts of the world some measure of freedom and stability are celebrated, but in other parts, civil unrest predominates. Such a dichotomy exists because the leaders of the places where freedom and stability are minimal or nonexistent are actively causing disintegration as they preoccupy themselves with bitter conflicts and wars. If conflict is now synonymous with Africa as expressed in Zewani's 1999 speech to the UN (Nhema 2004), then it is easy to conclude that many generations of Africans have never known what it means to live in peace and enjoy the liberties that make creativity possible. To comprehend this perspective, consider the plight of child soldiers and the condition of abducted children and women often routinely raped and abused. Also consider the consistent violence brought about by religious fundamentalism, armed conflict, brutal rebel groups, displaced populations leading to massive refugee crisis, and health challenges posed by diseases (HIV/AIDS, malaria, etc.).

These selected theories all clearly show that the behaviors and actions of presidents Gbagbo and Ouattara are explicable from different angles, and that such orchestrated behaviors are responsible for actions linked to grave consequences. In other words, from the theories, it is easier to perceive that political systems are socially constructed and given social significance. The impetus with which people politically and ideologically parade differing ways of life often propel actions that move people in directions that negate rumination about consequences. In the Ivoirian context, dictators barely spent time thinking about their actions. They simply assumed that years of oppression and subjugation of citizens into stifling docility was enough to maintain mass malleability to elite whims and control.

The internal corruptive theory comes out of the anger now rampant among African and Africanist scholars that African political elites and even members of the African upper class (not necessarily in government) are the sole perpetrators of the massive corruptions and disruptions that have driven the continent to its knees. The most vocal proponents of this theory are Soyinka (2005, 1996), Mbamara (2009), Ehusani (2002), and Chinua Achebe (Chinua Achebe Award Snub 2011) who point to the shortsightedness of African political and other leaders, and their extreme addiction to self-centeredness and insensitivity to fairness and civil society requirements. These scholars all paint a dismal picture of the continent made possible by cruel leadership and insist that any feel-good discourse that tries to portray an image of African nations getting better or rising from the ashes of their ruins is delusional at best as long as that behavior persists. These scholars insist that instead of blaming external forces (such as Western colonialism and neo-colonialism), it was time to recognize that African political and business elites were tearing the continent apart. Conversely, the negative behavior of ingrained corruptive behaviors and actions fragmenting the continent are being passed down to the younger generations.

Already in the late 1970s and early 1980s, even comedians and musicians such as Fela Kuti (Jaboro, 2012; Olaniyan 2004) completely understood that negative political leaders and their allies were deeply corrupted and fragmenting their individual nations. The theory concludes that the internal destructive behavior and actions of Africans themselves are to blame for the current conditions in Africa.

In using this theory to respond to the Côte d'Ivoire presidential crisis, it would appear that the Ivoirian political elite and its internal privileged allies brought the nation to its current conditions. The infighting from the moment Houphouët-Boigny died in office in 1993, through Bédié's presidency, all the way to the audacious claims made by Gbagbo after his defeat in the 2010 elections, are examples of corrupt individuals fighting for subjective control. They simply disregarded civility, the rule of law, democracy, and justice in order to enrich themselves rather than integrate the nation.

In protest, colonial, neo-colonial, and post-colonial theorists and historians, and some who insist there is even an eternal colonial dynamic in place (Benjamin and Hall 2010), would argue that the blame for disintegration, as well as the behavior and actions of political leaders in Africa, and all other colonized nations for that matter, cannot simply be attributed to internal conditions. For instance, one of the themes emphasized by some of the authors in Mazrui's edited work (Volume 8) of the UNESCO African history series focuses on European colonialism and imperialism and the powerful and destructive consequences they continue to have on the African continent (Mazrui 1999). However, Mazrui himself is also critical of the internal corruptive dynamics that have drained the continent of steam (Nation Correspondent 1998).

Questions such as, where did Ivoirian and other African leaders learn to be so selfish and divisive, and how they are able to sustain such unquestionable power remain unanswered by the internal corruptive theory. The colonial, post-colonial, and eternal colonial counterargument insists that a tragic socialization that is extremely difficult to erase was institutionalized by colonial logic and has been in place ever since, increasing in potency as generations of political leaders embrace it. A more dialectic perspective offered by Okosun (2010) is that the colonial and internal corruptive dynamics are intricately linked.

However, a recent populist piece from Ruwe (2012) titled "You Lazy (Intellectual) African Scum" sustains some of the arguments of the internal corruptive theory as it got Africans across the globe into a heated debate about (at least) recognizing that the numerous problems afflicting Africa nations were internally constructed. The internal corruptive theory may not be complete in terms of its ability to fully grasp national corruptive dynamics, but it helps to explain the challenges embedded in the behavior and actions of both Ivoirian presidents. It also helps with pointing to a self-recognition of culpability that is indispensable for Africans involved in intricate corruptive behaviors and actions that contribute to the disintegration of their continent. Since corruption is enlarged to include all kinds of adverse behavior and actions (embezzlement of finances, use of academic degrees to assume "big men" and "big women" positions rather than using them as tools to solve problems, disregard of civil society, and abuses of dignity and rights, to name a few), remedies may only be sought internally through intense longitudinal behavioral modifications.

Chapter Five

The Conflict through Social Cubism

The presidential conflict encompasses several deeply interconnected crucial conditions. Chapter 5 explores social cubism, a unique conflict model, to help create a deeper and more nuanced exploration of the different factors at play in the conflict.

THE CONFLICT THROUGH SOCIAL CUBISM

Social cubism is a conflict-mapping model. Its use here is specifically because the Ivoirian presidential conflict had some ethno-territorial dimensions. As a conflict-mapping model, social cubism examines conflict from a holistic rather than segmented stance. Social cubism's holistic approach is characterized by its six defined factors. These include historical, religious, economic, demographic, political, and psycho-cultural factors. These six factors work together to generate a better understanding of the interwoven forces that are often the causes or sources of conflict (Byrne and Carter 1996).

Côte d'Ivoire's political instability and conflict began in the 1980s and took some more eclectic turns in the late 1990s (McGovern 2011). Côte d'Ivoire, a West African nation, appeared to have been bitten by the bug of ethnic, religious, regional, and national challenges, augmented by the problem of dictatorships and military regimes. Civilian or military dictatorship is inappropriate for democratic and self-determining civil societies. In many African nations dictatorship is associated with brutality, ineptitude, shortsightedness, and dehumanization (Soyinka 1996, 2005).

Côte d'Ivoire was economically very successful during the Houphouët-Boigny era (1960s to early 1980s). Because of this success, not too many people openly questioned the homogenous philosophy of autocracy and dictatorship that undergirded the Ivoirian political system. Côte d'Ivoire was so successful that it was given the honor of housing the Africa Development Bank (ADB) in Abidjan. In addition, Ouattara, an Ivoirian with a PhD in economics, became an important leader of the Banque Centrale des Etats de l'Afrique de L'Ouest (BCEAO). It is possible that such success may have led to elite behaviors which abandoned civility to pursue personal gains.

Conversely, only Gbagbo (1982, 1983) could boldly tie the nature of the Ivoirian economy and politics to external manipulations (France). The inability to perceive the hands of France as a post-colonial power still active in Côte d'Ivoire offered a pseudo condition of economic and political independence. By 1999 (and this would continue well into early 2011), the political condition in Côte d'Ivoire had dramatically deteriorated with poor lower-stratum Ivoirians clearly excluded from political, economic, and social access (Aka 2006). This exclusion was intensified with Bédié's Ivoirité policy produced in 1994 (Toungara 2001), which Gbagbo tactically supported. Ivoirité persecuted Ivoirians who had Ivoirian and other West African parentage (heritage). The policy set off an ethnic negation and agitation that dragged the country into civil war in 2002 (Kouadio 2009). The following sections focus on a very brief description of the presidential conflict and its examination with the six factors of social cubism.

Brief Description of the Conflict

In Côte d'Ivoire, a number of circumstances paved the way for animosity between presidents Gbagbo and Ouattara. Gbagbo clearly had power and dominance, and used it throughout his presidency of almost ten years. From his perspective, there was really no conflict as such because Ouattara did not deserve to be contending for the presidency. Underlying this thought was the Ivoirité doctrine which already disqualified Ouattara since the time of Konan Bédié's presidency. Thus, not recognizing that the situation which had ensued was a major conflict clearly demonstrated the nature of Gbagbo's perception of power as something to be wielded at will to suit his whims.

When he was confronted by international pressure to appreciate the nature of the conflict, he rejected all invitation to reason. He used stalling tactics to prolong his inflexible position and sojourn in the presidency. His inflexibility was clearly relying on the Constitutional Court of Côte d'Ivoire (CCIC) and the military loyal to him as the final arbiter of the conflict. In West Africa, conflict resolution is often characterized by authoritarian imposition, violence, or in milder conditions, bribing the other party and its supporting members to shut up and go away. The groups with less power, usually smaller ethnic and religious groups, women, and those in the lower stratum, are often victimized by the common tactic of governance bodies peddling democracy and freedom, but once elected into office offering repression and subjugation (most West African governments are examples of this behavior).

Briefly, Gbagbo's interest in becoming the president of Côte d'Ivoire started in the late 1980s when he launched a series of thoughts on democracy and freedom, and actually challenged the benign dictator father of the nation, Houphouët-Boigny, in 1990. This critical stance against a powerful dictator empowered Gbagbo, who came back over and over in his attempt to rule Côte d'Ivoire. He finally succeeded in becoming president in 2000 and began to consolidate his sojourn as a powerful, autocratic, and dictatorial ruler. His refusal to allow elections revealed that he was planning to stay on as president indefinitely. When finally he conceded to elections in November of 2010, he had been in governance for ten years. Even then, Gbagbo hoped that the delay and prolonging tactics would turn the election in his favor. His tactic was much like that of Houphouët-Boigny (the father of the Ivoirian independent nation), to stay in power as long as possible so that the people become totally dependent on him while simultaneously distrusting of other contenders.

Ouattara, whose election had been prevented by Bédié, and now also Gbagbo, was running for the presidential position. Ouattara was, as it appeared to Gbagbo and his supporters, an outsider, who had spent much of his life abroad (in the West). He had been vilified as a half Ivoirian, and because Gbagbo defaulted to using the Ivoirité program for exclusionary reasons, he saw Ouattara as a foreigner and a Muslim, as well as an agent of the Western world who was trying to take an important political office from a legitimate and pure Ivoirian. Gbagbo was completely empowered when the first results of the elections came out. He was declared the winner. But electoral problems led to a second round of elections. When the final results of the 2010 elections came out, Ouattara was declared the winner. In disbelief, Gbagbo authorized the Ivoirian Supreme Court to reconfigure the election numbers and declare him the winner. The court did, and thus began the standoff between Gbagbo and Ouattara.

Having both declared themselves presidents of Côte d'Ivoire, a major presidential conflict was in full swing, and the scene was set for all kinds of internal and external diplomacy to effect either conflict management or transformation. It is understandable that Gbagbo would consider the second rounds of elections problematic (possibly rigged by Ouattara and his people), because he perceived himself as the winner in the first round. Moreover, the confidence which he had built up from his assumptions about power and control was too high to allow access to perceiving the possibility of losing the election. His solution was to default to his authoritative position and stay in power. Ouattara was simply satisfied that his campaign efforts had paid off, that Ivoirians could now perceive Gbagbo as an autocratic dictator, and that Ivorians would shift their allegiance to democracy and fairness. His victory was going to be vindicated in one way or another.

Presidents Gbagbo and Ouattara, the main parties of the conflict, each had a tremendous following among the Ivoirian population. Specifically, Ouattara had tremendous support from Ivoirians who felt they had been vilified and ostracized by years of Bédié's and Gbagbo's regimes. Other powerful stakeholders include the French government, the EU, the UN, the AU and the United States (considering that it had an African American leader). The United States especially was concerned that a collapsed Côte d'Ivoire may become one more haven for Islamic fundamentalists looking for bases in West Africa. This is understandable since the U.S. embassies in East Africa (Tanzania and Kenya) were unexpectedly bombed by Islamic fundamentalists in 1998.

Other stakeholders included powerful business elites within and outside the nation concerned about stability and business security. Gbagbo's contention was that democracy took time to be constituted in a nation that has only known dictatorship and coups, while Ouattara saw Gbagbo as the quintessential dictator shutting off all access to democracy and civility. It is ironic that both conflict parties talk about democracy, but their masculine and directional egos give pause as to what kind of democracy they were both peddling. In the history of colonial and independent West Africa, only the nation of Liberia has elected a female president (President Madame Ellen Johnson Sirleaf—see the story of Sirleaf in Cooper 2017). No matter how high women rose in the Ivoirian government, they have been openly excluded from the presidential office. Interestingly, Ouattara, more than Gbagbo, agreed that Côte d'Ivoire must not be allowed to disintegrate into chaos. Both were not interested in internal and/or external negotiations and diplomacy.

Both presidents retained firm political views sustained by immutable subjective constructs. Gbagbo insisted that his view of democracy mattered and was important for the eventual transformation of Côte d'Ivoire. Ouattara maintained that justice was not something that subjective whims can manipulate. In political processes, contenders often must give way to the decision of a fair electoral process. His argument was to place justice and fairness at the forefront of Ivoirian political experience. Thus, Ouattara's position was not to step down and concede defeat to a manipulative dictator, but to consolidate his presidency and get Gbagbo to step down gracefully without further damage to the nation.

For Ouattara, democracy, freedom, and self-determination required respecting the rule of law. While Gbagbo entrenched himself in the presidential palace, he continued to insist that he alone was the leader and center of political affairs. He let his supporters know that internal and external interference cannot detract from the presidency. Ouattara continued to point out that the practice of respecting the people's electoral votes is a civilized way of institutionalizing democracy. He viewed Gbagbo's insistence on staying in power as destructive to Ivoirians. Ouattara's position was that in order to get at a functional civil society, Ivoirians must be allowed to experience justice and the rule of law in action.

Both presidents' underlying interests point to the elements that are substantive in each party's concern. However, because this was a highly charged interpersonal conflict, interests may have been confused with positions. Wilmot and Hocker (2007, 258–259) point out that positions generally diminish the possibility of agreement, while interests enable conflict parties to focus on elements that are mutable yet substantively crucial. Also, Wehr (1979, 24) points out that sometimes (depending on the conflict) interest, ideology, and value can get easily confused.

Gbagbo's position, which may easily be confused with an interest, was that no one was fit to be president but himself. In order to protect this position by all means against internal and external forces, he invoked a hyper-dictatorial posture to sustain his continued tenure in the presidency. Ouattara had both a position and an interest. His position was to protect his dignity and right to the presidency, and since he viewed Gbagbo to be an irrational and dangerous man, he refused to negotiate with him, claiming there was no basis for such action. His interest was to secure justice and fairness, and by so doing reinstate Côte d'Ivoire as a working democracy. Ouattara was also concerned about the nature of economic and social conditions, which deteriorated during Gbagbo's tenure, and so was interested in a government that stabilized conditions. The rest of this section on social cubism turns to the six factors in view of the conflict between presidents Gbagbo and Ouattara.

History Factors

Contentions about history have primarily focused on whose history is significant and documentable and whose is insignificant and to be omitted. Since history is significant in getting at the source of conflict, it is useful here to name the origin of at least most of the elements that brought about the presidential conflict.

The historical factors reveal that several complex elements were at play. The distinct populations of Upper Volta (now Burkina Faso) and Côte d'Ivoire were brought together by colonial France. After Côte d'Ivoire gained independence, some of Upper Volta continued on its own as a separate nation, later renaming itself Burkina Faso. The rest of the northern population was merged with Côte d'Ivoire to form one nation that was mostly Islamic and continued to practice that faith. However, in contemporary Côte d'Ivoire, the southerners (mostly Christians and interspersed with negligible indigenous and Islamic religious folks) dominate political, economic, and social affairs, and even though Muslim influences have contributed to the development of Côte d'Ivoire, the northerners have had a harder time in terms of accessing egalitarian treatment.

The Ivoirité doctrine established by President Bédié created a distinction between "pure blood" Ivoirians (both parents verified as authentic Ivoirians) and individuals with one parent from Côte d'Ivoire and the other parent from a different nation. The Ivoirité program was devastating to Ivoirians who had both an Ivoirian and another heritage such as Ghana, Liberia, Sierra Leone, Guinea, Mali, Nigeria, and Benin. Thus Bédié's action created a stifling and divisive socio-political context. Gbagbo, a political outsider, who studied and lived in France, returned to teach history at a university in Côte d'Ivoire and was supposed to be "cultured," but he took advantage of Ivoirité to sustain his own presidential agenda (see Q&A: Ivory Coast Crisis 2011).

It is useful to point out that Gbagbo's scholarly effort from the 1980s to the 1990s was dedicated to exploring the impact of colonization and the usefulness of democracy for Côte d'Ivoire. He successfully challenged President Houphouët-Boigny (who stayed in power for more than thirty years, was from the Boaulé ethnic group, and had populated the government with his ethnic group). Gbagbo was from one of the two dominant ethnic groups, the Krou and Kwa. He was from the Krou group and was specifically Bété. Bédié, the notorious president before Gbagbo, was from the Kra ethnic group, which he openly argued was best suited for governance (Skogseth 2006). The problem with having dominant ethnic groups in governance is their entrenchment in political office. Even though they experience intra-group conflict, dominant groups always ensure that they stay in power.

Ouattara, a Muslim and from the northern region of the nation, was a political insider who was handpicked by Houphouët-Boigny to rectify the nation's economic woes in 1990 and later appointed prime minister. President Houphouët-Boigny's "Open Door" policy ensured diversity of representation in the government. Bédié was also handpicked by Houphouët-Boigny and made the head of the Ivoirian parliament. It is not entirely clear why he picked both men. Perhaps they were picked and groomed in Houphouët-Boigny's benign dictatorial governance philosophy with the hope that they would eventually head the Ivoirian government playing different but important roles. What is clear is that President Houphouët-Boigny was comfortable with the input of all members of the Ivoirian society as long as they were anointed by him.

When President Houphouët-Boigny died in office in 1993, Ouattara's attempts to claim the presidential office were repelled by Bédié's invocation of the constitution which claimed that the head of the Ivoirian parliament was the rightful successor in the event of such an incident. Bédié's presidency was filled with socio-political divisiveness, and he was finally forced out by General Guéï's military coup in 1999. During this period, coups had become internalized in West African behavior. Guéï was a total disaster, and Gbagbo's accession into the presidency drained civility to its nadir. Arguably, Ouattara's anger against Bédié and later Gbagbo may be justifiable considering that he was shut out of the presidential process by people he considered dubious individuals who used divisive ideologies and clearly preferred dictatorship rather than service to citizens.

In summary, the historical dimension of the conflict shows its complexity. First, Gbagbo and Ouattara are participants in a chain of events that started before they were born. The colonial actions that brought two differing populations together, and the authoritarian doctrine that sustained dictatorial rule after independence, created an inflexible political elite. Second, subjective positions were quickly formed as it became clear that political office and the use of governance power had interminable benefits. Subjective ideologies turned Ivoirian elites against each other in ways that became damaging to the nation. Third, subsequent presidents sought to sustain only the conditions that benefited them as the complexity of governing Côte d'Ivoire increased polarization and civil crisis, as well as infrastructure and development issues. The obvious consequence is the collapse of the justice system. Fourth, women were overtly excluded from presidential governance. Since independence women had never been positioned as top leaders. The missed opportunity drove a wedge between the egalitarianism of women and men. Fifth, the internalization of political elitism gave space for stifling ethnic and class cultures that quickly separated Ivoirians from each other. Thus, the chain of events which began with Houphouët-Boigny's death in 1993 was also linked to external stakeholders, especially the Western world, which needed to guarantee that natural resources (cocoa, coffee, petroleum) were never going to stop flowing or fall into the hands of "rogues or factional nations" in the event that Côte d'Ivoire became a failed state. In a failed state such as Somalia, chaos and anarchy dominate, and safety and security of citizens and international commerce within and around it become issues of grave concern (Eichstaedt 2010).

Religious Factors

The religious dimension allows people to coalesce around specific doctrinal practices which, in turn, influence their social and other worldviews. For instance, even in the dating world, some people are not satisfied with finding just any mate; they seek a "Christian" or "Muslim" or "Hindu" one. This means that the religious dimension encourages people to populate in preferred and deliberately selected social contexts. This is true for Côte d'Ivoire, with Christians populating the South and Muslims populating the North. As well, even though Ivoirians mostly view themselves as either Christian or

Muslim (Langer 2005), there are still specks of Ivoirian traditional religions which pre-date both Christianity and Islam (Skogseth 2006).

The nature of the diversity of religions is not specifically a problem; rather, it is the polarization that religious adherents insert into interactions with each other. The Christians often view the Muslims as trying to proselytize and convert Ivoirians to Islam. The Christians' general perception is that Islam is a problem religion. The Christians, especially the ones with "missionary attitudes," continue to try to convert Muslims and traditional African religious believers into various groups of Christianity because they argue that Islam and African traditional religions are hopeless in the scheme of "true salvation."

Quite astonishingly, traditional African religions do not have missionary or conversion programs. Instead, they are content with the enjoyment of their complex experiences. But beyond proselytizing and conversion, religious groups intimidate each other. The larger and more dominant the group, the more power it wields and seeks. One of the critical factors within the Ivoirian religious scene is that political leaders also use religion to mark those who can serve in government. Religion in this sense plays a huge role in who gets selected for what office. It is not surprising that Ouattara had a hard time gaining the presidency because of his religion (Islam) and regional affiliation (northerner connected to Islam).

In socio-political arrangements, the religious dimension has become a powerful force in West Africa, often manifesting as the source of national and intergroup conflict. In Nigeria, for instance, the Boko Haram (the name means Western education is sacrilegious), an Islamic group, continues in a long tradition of fighting Christians for political power and control of the nation (Who are Nigeria's Boko Haram 2016). Even though it is only a negligible Islamic sect, it does not like the diversity of religions and social experiences, hence its desire to Islamize Nigeria (Who are Nigeria's Boko Haram 2016).

The colonial decision in Nigeria to amalgamate two disparate groups, the North (mostly Islamized and indigenous religions) and the South (mostly Christianized and indigenous religions) in 1914 (Falola and Heaton 2008) into one nation led to a civil war (1966–1970), coups, and continued struggle for power by both groups. This is somewhat similar to the Ivoirian scenario. In Côte d'Ivoire, presidents Gbagbo and Ouattara were in a complex interpersonal conflict with high religious and national implications. Moreover, the insistence of Bédié and Gbagbo on referring to Ouattara as a foreigner in a nation with about 25 or more percent of "foreigners" (see Langer 2005, 30) was clearly hinged on portraying him as having an ethnicity and a religion that did not fit what they perceived as the "true Ivoirian" context.

Demographic Factors

The population of Côte d'Ivoire is ethnically and religiously diverse. As of 2016, the Ivoirian population peaked at approximately 23.9 million people which include the following ethnic groups: Akan 29 percent, the Gur 16 percent, the Mandes (North) 15 percent, the Mandes (South) 10 percent, the Krus 9 percent, and others, including Lebanese and French living in Côte d'Ivoire. Also all Christians comprise approximately 34 percent, Muslims 43 percent, and indigenous religions 4 percent, and so on. Foreign migratory workers comprise approximately 73 percent Muslims and Christians 18 percent (Central Intelligence Agency 2017). Moreover, several immigrant groups and their languages include Bisa (63,000), Dogoso, Eastern Karaboro (5,610), Glaro-Twabo, Jenaama Bozo, Khe, Malba Birifor, Mòoré, Siamou, Sìcìté Sénoufo, Soninke (100,000), Southern Toussian, Turka, and Vietnamese (Simons and Fennig 2017). This demographic distribution is important because it shows the diversity of ethnic and religious groups in Côte d'Ivoire.

However, it is useful to point out that even though the Muslim population is clearly the majority, they are overwhelmed by the political dominance of the Kwa and Kru ethnic groups who are politically dominant. To keep Muslims and other groups subjugated, Bédié once commented that the Kwa were better suited for political governance (Skogseth 2006). Traditionally, the ruling group was mostly Boaulé, Houphouët-Boigny's group, but with the coming of Bédié (Kwa) and Gbagbo (Kru), more individuals of their groups entered the elite ranks.

In addition, the high Muslim immigrant population working in both the cocoa fields and the Abidjan port has been a source of contestation. Some of Gbagbo's people were involved in intimidating some of the immigrant communities who formed the farming communities. The intimidation was based on the perception that the immigrants did not belong in Côte d'Ivoire (see Kouadio 2009; see also Akindès 2003). As well, colonial France has much to do with the current demographic arrangements and the circumstances in which different groups experience themselves as Ivoirians. Frantz Fanon (1965) did not mince words when he exposed the brutality of the French in North Africa. Even though Fanon's work was in North Africa (Algeria specifically), the brutality was endemic to other colonial contexts such as Haiti, Cameroun, Senegal, and Vietnam. Much of the brutality involved physical harms and forcing differing ethnic groups to merge and become one unit under French control.

Finally, in Côte d'Ivoire, major ethnic groups with political power have tremendous control which causes problems for less dominant groups and women in general. An interesting dimension of the demographic factor is that the two presidents both unquestioningly counted on the power of their constituencies to get them to the presidency. Strongly nestled in the discourse of demographic politics is the idea that Gbagbo counted heavily on the power of his ethnic group (Kru) and other supporters, and the weight of his regional affiliation to the South of Côte d'Ivoire to guarantee his win in 2010. Ouattara aimed for the same thing with a twist. He counted on the entire North, the Muslim population, and sympathizers in the South to get him to the presidency.

Political Factors

Civil societies generally support and sustain good governance and political systems. This means that politically, people and constituencies ought to collaborate with one another if they are to achieve and anchor social stability. This includes respect for voting laws and for the distribution of common goods and services so that everyone has fair, equal access. In addition, all government systems should maintain components of legitimacy, and for this, social justice or distributive justice is indispensable. Of course, without good governance conflict can erupt at any time. More than good governance, the distribution of political offices is extremely important so that each group within the nation feels adequately represented.

In the past (1960s–1980s) Ivoirians had good working relationships with each other, the economy was great, and citizens were somewhat proud of their nation. The political powder keg that ignited the presidential conflict was the mentality of the successive leaders (mostly southern) after Houphouët-Boigny, who allowed subjective, corruptive, greedy, and ethnocentric propensities to dominate governance. In other words, by concentrating power in a few dominant groups' hands, democracy and civil society were surreptitiously (some would argue overtly) siphoned out of Côte d'Ivoire.

Finally, the political factors consider infighting, jockeying for power, and the use of violence as a major catalyst for distrust, as well as increased anger and antagonism. Also important is the link to the international community, and the international community's determination to have the conflict resolved. Whereas Gbagbo saw the international community as meddling with internal affairs, Ouattara, an economic expert, saw the need for good global interaction which maintains good standing before the IMF, the World Bank, the UN, and to a lesser extent, the AU and ECOWAS.

In political arrangements, even though women were not out there in the pool of candidates running for top government positions, it is imaginable that they were in the background fueling their husbands, sons, and friends to defend their turfs with all it takes. However, the consistent exclusion of women from specifically presidential-level participation adds to the latent political factors.

Since there were two contending political agendas, it was difficult for Ivoirians to understand which was best during the presidential conflict. While Gbagbo exhibited dictatorial propensities, he was also beyond caring about saving face (he refused the United States' offer for asylum) as he positioned himself for a long battle. The lengthier the battle, the worse things got. Ouattara, on the other hand, had actually run Côte d'Ivoire when he was prime minister. During his tenure, the economy began to pick up. In the presidential conflict, and unlike Gbagbo, he did not want Côte d'Ivoire to disintegrate into total chaos. Such chaos would cause it to lose legitimacy before the international community. This was a fundamental recognition that internal political configuration cannot be estranged from external political interactions. This perception was perhaps one of the many reasons why Ouattara proceeded to use violence to shut the conflict down.

Economic Factors

For societies to thrive, they need a good economic system. Much of the time populations rely on good economics to be able to upgrade their lives. Bad economics or the manipulation of economics by a few elites to their advantage at the expense of others often leads to disastrous consequences. Overall, economics requires interaction, continuity, and a fair system of government and private systems to sustain it. Since it is the process whereby people produce and exchange goods, its viability depends entirely on good governance which produces functioning and responsible public policy that undergirds all economic activities. This means that the ethical dimension of good economics relies very much on everyone responding to the fair distributive model, the kind argued for by Rawls (1971, 2001), Barry (2005), and Nathanson (1998). It is especially useful that the social cubism model draws economic factors into its conflict mapping because all elements of economics continue to be significant players in the generation of social conflict.

In Côte d'Ivoire, the inequality between the wealthy, the political elite, and the poor is extremely high. The military coups that occurred there resulted from economic conditions. One of the many reasons for the first coup in 1999 was a demand by the military for payment of services rendered in peacekeeping activities. The second coup in 2002 and the civil war that followed occurred because President Gbagbo (following in President Bédié's footsteps) had stifled economic options for northerners and many other Ivoirians. As people became more empowered to take action in view of survival, riots and violence caused more economic misery to members of the lower stratum who live on less than two dollars a day (World Bank, 2011). The elite and wealthy populations were generally well-protected by internal and external powers. For instance, when a coup or a major violent event is about to occur, powerful elites circulate such information among themselves, giving enough time for members to escape to Europe, the United States, or elsewhere. Those caught off guard are usually the opponents of the perpetrators and the mass of poor citizens.

It is interesting that while Gbagbo and Ouattara were in conflict, the negotiators who convened in the attempt to resolve the conflict spent enormous monies to feast and entertain elite participants, while many Ivoirians experienced food, medicine, and other shortages. Both presidents insisted on two very different economic programs. Gbagbo became anti-external economic and political interference, while Ouattara craved such a relationship as the only way out of the Ivoirian economic quagmire.

Measures that were taken to respond to the crisis also had an effect on economic stability. It is rare that wealthy elites would sacrifice their economic privileges and benefits in order to help support those suffering or to help prop up the nation in a time of crisis. What is common is the looting of the national treasury and exit to Western or other nations where enough monies have been stashed away for such a contingency. Because the presidential conflict caused tremendous fear, diminished income, absence of wages and labor opportunities, and food shortages, populations in the lower stratum of the Ivoirian society were mostly those who suffered, were displaced, ended up as refugees, or simply had nowhere to go.

Psycho-cultural Factors

Psycho-cultural dynamics became a threatening source of social conflict when dominant groups insisted that their cultural foundations and experiences were superior to those of less dominant groups. The inverse is that less dominant groups also look to their own cultural identity as a way to solidify their presence and seek inclusion. Whichever ways they emerged, psycho-cultural factors became a grave source of social conflict in Côte d'Ivoire.

The presidential conflict resulted in in-group as well as out-group formalization of perceptions. President Gbagbo and his supporters insisted on sustaining their position through the imposition of power, coercion, recognition, and familiarity. They positioned the idea of a Muslim leader as threatening, psychologically demoralizing, and culturally problematic. The ideological machine spun rumors that with a Muslim president the Muslim North of the country will become more empowered to overrun the nation. On the other hand, Ouattara and his supporters, and even neutral internal and external observers, pointed out that worse psycho-cultural trauma awaits Côte d'Ivoire if dictatorship is allowed to flourish. Dictatorship will simply mean the end of democracy, the end of justice and fairness, and the end of a true representative government. Beyond these, the demoralizing conditions that the presidential conflict visited on every Ivoirian created a wedge between healing from past strife, for instance the civil war and years of ethnic divisiveness, and moving forward to new expectations.

To conclude the discussion on exploring the presidential conflict with the social cubism model, globalization theory is a useful response to social cubism. Consider that Côte d'Ivoire was very successful in the 1960s and 1970s and so was a child of the early form of globalization. Bhagwati (2006) insists that globalization has been generally good, and that specifically, it has positively affected the lives of many disadvantaged populations. Echoing this view is Stiglitz (2002) who points out that globalization could be a good force when it is not configured in such a way that only the core nations (European-populated regions of the globe) profit from it. Yet globalization has also been devastating (Bauman 1998).

Its impact in Côte d'Ivoire may be the result of the economic problems that overtook the country in the 1980s. For this reason, globalization theory may view social cubism to be missing an element, namely global trends, which needs to be added to its six determinants. That is, it would insist that trying to map the presidential conflict in terms of the six elements is not enough in a world where global trends and their vast and sophisticated powers have become encompassing, forceful, and homogenizing.

This means that the presidential conflict in Côte d'Ivoire was the function of extremely complex and encompassing global forces that uncontrollably swung internal conditions in so many adverse directions. In this configuration, the marriage of Ivoirian political elites and globalization most probably supplied the coup de grâce. Both the politicians and globalization have no boundaries; neither do they have compassion for weaker citizens. Their marriage survives on a complex algorithmic internal logic of greed and lawlessness. As the presidential conflict imposed fear and uncertainly, the conflict parties spoke in terms of reimagining the nation with democracy and prosperity, code words for markets and economy. Ivoirian socio-economic and socio-political conditions cannot exist without global interactions.

Instead of social cubism relying on the six factors to map the presidential conflict, globalization theory would argue that a seventh factor, global trends, may enhance the picture of the conflict so as to place Côte d'Ivoire in a global mono-cultural context. In this mono-cultural context, the specific discontents of globalization which have manifested in many poor countries across the globe cannot be discounted (Stiglitz 2002).

In the context of discontent, Shiva (1993) and Bauman (1998) show that homogenizing and mono-culturalizing disparate poorer nations into a global convenience store or marketplace are only advantageous to dominant powerful nations. The global convenience store forces poor nations into a sham economic and other interactive relationship with dominant nations. That relationship leads to internal economic struggles within the poor nations triggered by dominant global trends. The outcomes of these trends often lead to civil strife as political elites struggle to control people, labor, the military, and resources with the privileges that come with them. Some globalization theorists would, therefore, complement social cubism by adding that the presidential conflict in Côte d'Ivoire is part of a complex global maze of sophisticated activities where internal powers, perpetually hinged to external powers and hyper-conglomerates, fight over the control of conditions that are in some ways beyond their control. Clearly, the idea of linking globalization theory to social cubism's theoretical mapping enhances the explanation of the Ivoirian presidential conflict's multi-dimensional internal and external dynamics.

Chapter Six

Dictator Behavior

Major socio-political and socio-economic problems began showing up in Côte d'Ivoire in the late 1980s. These problems intensified after the death of President Houphouët-Boigny (1993) and continued to increase during Gbagbo's presidency.

Most nations rely on good governance and the positive uses of political power for all kinds of advancement. However, poor governance and the negative use of political power portend devastation to most citizens and to the national character of any nation. Over the years, identities such as race, ethnicity, religion, gender, sexuality, class, and nationality have been used to define how privileges, advantages, deservingness, and undeservingness are apportioned in many local and global contexts. Several examples of individual or collective negative uses of political power abound.

Consider the European mass enslavement and harm of Africans. Also, the massive destruction of millions of people during World Wars I and II was fueled by fascism, nationalism, Nazism, and imperialism. The dehumanizing Jim Crow laws (circa 1868–1968) and the virulent apartheid system of South Africa (Terreblanche 2002) all insisted that African Americans and Africans (who did nothing but good) had to be subdued under the dehumanizing socially constructed rules of supremacy and utter "racial" hatred. The negative use of political power was present in Chile during the Pinochet regime and in many other Latin American contexts. As well, this negative political behavior was evident in Myanmar, North Korea, and several African nations.

An excellent example of disguised and current negative use of political power is found in the repressive new Jim Crow Laws (post-1968 to present) in the United States. The new disguised Jim Crow system tactically reenslaves millions of African Americans through mass incarceration (Alexander 2010). In addition, this behavior is now dominant in the recent resurgence of negative nationalism, religious and racial bigotry, and racial supremacy, all reempowered through national political platforms (see elections and uses of political power in the United States, and in some EU nations between 2016 through 2020).

As for Côte d'Ivoire, the nature of polarization using ethnicity, religion, class, and national status emerged shortly after independence, and thereafter internalized itself into social and political affairs and behavior. Such polarization as infused inflexible absolutism into the uses of political power, conditioning many leaders and even citizens to opt for harmful negation of each other. In a way, dictator behavior seeks to infect ordinary citizens with negativity so that they become antagonistic to each other in every way possible. When citizens are divided into bitter opposing camps and turned against each other, dictators use the chaos that ensues as an opportunity to entrench themselves in power.

Nigeria, for instance, suffered through a major civil war known as the Nigeria-Biafra War (1966-1970) (Nkwocha 2010; Uzokwe 2003), military coups, brutal dictators, and corrupt civilian regimes. Each successive regime used ethnic and religious discontent and polarization to get into and stay in power. Several West African nations, including Côte d'Ivoire, have experienced similar challenges. Critical internal strife has a deep and lasting effect on the socialization and perceptions of citizens. Contemporary Africans across the globe have deep-seated distrust of governance and political systems. Instead, they want positive and productive socio-economic and socio-political changes.

The assumption for good governance and positive use of political power is that citizens give a mandate to political representatives to create and ensure equal opportunity and a functional distributive justice scheme. This means that political power is important in the sense that it is useful in sustaining social, economic, social-justice, and political dynamics within any nation. Good governance and positive political power are tied to good leadership behaviors in view of a civil society where citizens' well-being comes first.

Drawing from the extensive agitations across Côte d'Ivoire, it is clear that political leaders became distracted from responsibilities to the common good. Instead, and for years, they focused on bitter battles against each other to sustain subjective personal benefits. The Gbagbo-Ouattara presidential conflict gives further insight into dictatorial behavior. While they used promissory socio-political language to engage the Ivoirians and global communities, they were inadvertently focused on their own subjective benefits. This focus clearly marked sequences of neglect and abandonment of those governed, specifically the lower stratum of the society.

Karl Marx constructed a socio-economic and socio-political analysis of the causes of conflict in society. Marx critically evaluated history and found within it a careful organization of exploitative systems formalized by the deliberate efforts of a few wealthy and powerful people. These individuals, whom he dubbed the bourgeois, postulated themselves as superior and deserving people over the rest of the local and global population of the time. Marx's critical historical examination encompassed the events and behavior of wealthy and elite Europeans, which had tremendous impact on Europe, the New World in the Americas, and the colonized populations of the African, Asian, and Polynesian continents. Conversely, the bourgeois, fully immersed in capitalism—a newfound justification for greed and complete social apathy—heaped all forms of disadvantages on the masses of poor people (see Marx 1934).

From the historical critical point of view, Marx was perhaps the first scholar to critically delineate that history is not a natural phenomenon, but rather something deliberately organized and orchestrated by human beings. As he saw it then, history was subjective, selective, and exclusive. During his time, historical events were already replete with the deliberate separation of people into the haves and the have-nots. The bourgeois emerged as the winners in history, and the masses of people would always remain subservient to these winners, their whims, and desires. This, of course, means that Marx's critical reading of history had clearly delineated the problem of massive social inequality and exploitation which he argued was the source of the conflict between the bourgeois and the masses, and must not be left unchecked for fear that a predetermined course of historical inequality would manifest itself eternally.

In 1867, Marx was able to show in his *Capital* (1934) that historical evidence predisposed the masses to systemic social and economic exclusion. Marx's reasoning at this time was quite significant because history had clearly demonstrated that powerful kings and/or leaders (from great African, European, and Asian super leaders) had configured governance and social advantages in their own favor. For instance, even when what seemed like a solution emerged to give people (not to the king) rule-making power, the nobles and clergy of England who forced King John (c. 1215 CE) to accept the Magna Carta and a parliamentary system still found a way to insert themselves as beneficiaries of power (see Danziger and Gillingham 2004). Conversely by the 1800s, despotic kings, nobles, and clergy were being edged out by greedy and despotic capitalists, whose main interest was to exploit docile masses of people for cheap labor. The outcome of minimizing human beings and exploiting their labor was the massive increased wealth and lavish lifestyles, which the bourgeois and their allies enjoyed.

Moving from Marx's analysis, it was not until the 1940s and 1950s that colonized and dehumanized populations began to examine historical events in relation to their own conditions. These critical examinations led to sociopolitical movements, which in turn, led to the independence of several colonized groups. Unfortunately, the tragic cyclic liberator-to-dictator phenomenon would envelop the leaders of newly liberated nations. Although nations freed themselves from despotic colonizers, the elite members of these new nations had quickly become despotic, merciless, and autocratic rulers.

By the early 1960s, a few scholars (mostly liberation theologians) with new interests in the implication of historical actions for the human condition began to ask deeper questions. Many of these scholars critically focused on history and some of the popular and immutable texts used to sustain it, and began naming the sources of harms in the human experiences of the past and current daily conditions. For this new group of critical historical-social scholars, exploited and forgotten people—discarded as nonentities by coercive governments and apathetic elites and their allies—had to be brought back to life and postulated as dignified and deserving of rights and privileges denied them. These daring efforts added dynamic prescriptions such as the need for restoration and liberation, and in some cases, transformation (Mahatma Gandhi, Martin Luther King Jr., and so on) so that those forced into historical oblivion such as subordinated nations, the poor, racial and ethnic groups, women, the disappeared, and the marginalized, oppressed, and/or repressed in various ways, would be vindicated.

In the light of this critical questioning, human actions within history were linked to the conditions of suffering and marginalization. Popularizing this analysis were Martin Luther King Jr. (1958), Stokely Carmichael and Charles Hamilton (1967), Camilo Torres (1968), James Cone (1969, 1970), Gustavo Gutiérrez (1973), Enrique Dussel (1978, 1979, 1980), Ellacuría (1980, 1987, 1989), Romero (1981), Ellacuría and Sobrino (1990), Paulo Freire (1990), and many others in liberation theology and philosophy circles. These scholars employed a nuanced and more textured version of analysis to chart a path which illuminated history by simultaneously exposing past and present forms of oppression, exploitation, marginalization, and violence.

It is interesting that in about 1963, the Reverend Father Camilo Torres, a Roman Catholic priest was so upset with dictatorial governance system in Colombia that he took up arms with a group of priests (Padres Diego Cristobal Uribe, Antonio Jimenez, Domingo Lain, and Manuel Perez Martinez) to fight against repression and oppression. They entered the jungles of Colombia to support the first guerrilla movement against the Colombian autocratic and dictatorial governing bourgeois. During the 1950 through the 1990s, many governments across the globe acted with repressive impunity over their own citizens. Many of these governments overtly or subtly disregarded the positive uses of governance and political power in favor of dictatorial, repressive, and subjective agendas.

The actions of the two feuding presidents in Côte d'Ivoire added a critical piece to the nature of autocracy and dictatorship. Regardless of whether dictators are content or threatened, democracy, civil society, and social justice suffer. The impact of their negative uses of governance and political power in their different regions of the world have been devastating (see the aforementioned activists, as well as Lutuli 1962; Nyerere 1968; Rodney 1972; Moore 1973; Biko and Stubbs 1978). For Côte d'Ivoire, the impact of the presidential conflict, which highlighted autocratic and dictatorial behavior, included using negative ethnic and religious sentiments, as well as exclusionary politics, to coerce Ivoirians into the negation of each other. This polarization increased social disintegration wherein poverty, violence, and other desperate conditions coalesced.

The presidential conflict was complex. The behaviors of President Gbagbo refusing to relinquish power after he lost the election and the insistence of Alassane Ouattara, who refused to relinquish his election victory underscore the complexity of autocratic behavior. Ouattara viewed Gbagbo as an autocrat trying to reactivate dictatorship in Côte d'Ivoire. Adding to the complexity were the series of internal, regional, continental, and other international efforts which tried to help with negotiations between the two presidents in order to stabilize Côte d'Ivoire. Because of the nondemocratic condition and the presence of the symptoms of dictatorial behavior, President Ouattara ended the conflict with military violence. Ouattara was supported by France (old colonial master), the UN Security Council, and the NF troops (linked to the former rebel leader Guillame Soro). Ironically, Soro was once Gbagbo's peace-brokered prime minister. Soro resigned and joined the Ouattara camp when Gbagbo refused to leave office.

There were a number of impacts evident from the presidential conflict. Many schools were closed, so there was no continuity in education. Other challenges include the absence of good healthcare services and transportation. There were divisions between women and men, ethnic groups, and religions. Even basic resources such as shelter, food, sanitary systems, water, electricity, labor, and wage payments were difficult to fulfill. Specifically noteworthy are religion and ethnicity, because access to common resources was possible or hampered depending on citizens' affiliation.

INCREASED POLARIZATION

The Problem of Ivoirité

Increased polarization between ethnic and social groups became extreme before the presidential conflict (Skogseth 2006; Konaté 2005; Copnall 2004; Pawson 2004; Akindès 2003; Scheuer and Trembloy 2001) and completely polarized the nation during the presidential conflict (Zouande 2011; Besnahan 2011). During Bedie's presidential tenure (1993–1999), Ivoirité law (created in 1994), was systematically used to create and stir up ethnic and religious differences (Toungara 2001). These differences led to the most devastating divisiveness in Côte d'Ivoire (Zouande 2011; McGovern 2011;

Kouadio 2009). Specifically, the most interesting thing about Ivoirité is that it became a national tool used by some Ivoirians to discriminate and construct access to deservingness against each other (Zouande 2011; Skogseth 2006; Akindès 2003). General Guéï, who overthrew Bédié in 1999 and was only in power for less than one year, also used it to his advantage (Chirot 2006). Gbagbo used Ivoirité and increased all kinds of tension. During the presidential conflict with Ouattara, drumming up Ivoirité sentiments helped increase the national polarization that firmly divided Ivoirians into disparate groups (Zouande 2011).

In this scenario, where Ivoirians were negatively empowered against each other, a number of adverse social conditions such as poverty, food shortages, and refugee/people displacement issues manifested. These adverse conditions increased for the weaker ethnic, religious, "half citizens," and immigrant groups who were targeted and demonized by proponents of Ivoirité, as well as adherents of other political and nationalistic ideologies. Ironically, the demonization occurred within adverse social conditions, which had gone way beyond just ethnic and religious configurations, to include complex socio-political and socio-economic dynamics (Meehan 2011). The combination of massive social justice issues such as Ivoirians experiencing food shortages, the presence of international and internal aid workers trying to help, and the massive number of refugees from Côte d'Ivoire asking for help from neighboring nations (Liberia, Guinea, and Burkina Faso) all point to the kinds of complex socio-political problems tied into increased polarization.

In volatile conflict scenarios, even when people are equally poor, the poor group that feels dominant still persecutes all other groups. This is more of a socio-political behavior than it is a condition directly linked to any group of people. Increased aggression on the part of the poor, especially in terms of being merciless to each other, is one of several outcomes of social polarization. Rwanda is an example of a conflict scenario where mostly the poor unwittingly butchered other poor members of society because of complex political dynamics that locked them into ethnic, socio-economic, and socio-political polarization. In addition, the unchecked extreme power on the part of one group of poor people (mostly institutionalized by socio-political factors and then taken advantage of by the elite) and its brutal use of that power either increases anger on the part of other groups being vilified or creates total fear, intimidation, and submission.

However, because they are both poor, the oppressor and the oppressed generally suffer through the same social problems that emerge from such social chaos. The ethnic, religious, social, and political polarization clearly heightened vertical inequalities in the lower stratum, as well as in the elite communities (Langer 2005). By separating themselves from each other and then vilifying each other, Gbagbo and Ouattara gave clear indication of vertical inequality which stretched the polarization farther during the conflict.

The lower stratum, also searching for social justice and political reparation, simply sided with either Gbagbo or Ouattara and used their political positions and ideologies to hurt each other (Allen 2011; James 2010).

Within the problem of Ivoirité, polarization is specifically linked to a very important element, namely food shortages which affected most Ivoirians (James 2010). In addition and because of the crisis, food prices increased (James 2010). In this scenario, only those who could afford such prices bought whatever food was available.

Food shortages intensified as both presidents took various actions to consolidate their power. For instance, Gbagbo's ardent supporters, the "Young Patriots," the military, and other clandestine mafia-type groups increased the level of fear and intimidation in the society. Much like in the 2000s after the civil strife, these mostly young males paraded the streets of Abidjan and other southern areas with impunity, setting up checkpoints indiscriminately and intimidating Ivoirians and immigrants who they perceived were Ouattara followers.

Within the problem of Ivoirité, uncertainty emerged as an aspect of polarization. Within the context of uncertainty, looting, vandalism, and infrastructural damage persisted during the conflict and continued after the conflict (IRIN 2011). Ouattara's supporters, members of the FRCI and their support militia, angry about previous social arrangements that disenfranchised and vilified them, targeted and killed Gbagbo supporters in the Western town of Duekoue on March 28, 2011 (Doyle 2011; Amnesty International 2011). Gbagbo supporters also unleashed their anger on Ouattara's people (Amnesty International 2011).

When people are uncertain about social conditions, it follows that the society has no signals for clear substantive predictions about resolution and getting back to normalcy. Uncertainty creates the atmosphere of fear, resulting in Ivoirians fleeing the country (Q&A: Ivory Coast Crisis 2011). Before the presidential crisis, neighboring countries (especially Burkina Faso) were ready to receive Ivoirian refugees (Chirot 2006). This is because most of the northern Ivoirians have generational relatives connected to Burkina Faso. In 2010, this was also expected, but in addition to Burkina Faso, Liberia, Guinea, and even Mali expected an inflow of displaced people from Côte d'Ivoire.

Uncertainty also increased when Ouattara, supported by the United Nation, AU, and France, mandated the use of force to take Gbagbo out (United Nations Security Council 2011b). The atrocities committed by supporters of both Ouattara and Gbagbo (Doyle 2011) raised several concerns not only about the senseless violence but also about continued violence during the post-conflict scenario. For instance, even though the civil strife ended in April 11, 2011, uncertainty still lingered for many of Gbagbo's supporters because they were unsure of their new condition now that Ouattara was the president of the nation (Doyle 2011). After the conflict, some of them switched allegiance to President Ouattara to avoid persecution, but the die-hard Gbagbo supporters continued to cause problems here and there (United Nations Security Council 2011a). However, even after Gbagbo was ousted, the post-conflict scenario was not quite tempered yet. There was uncertainty at the personal and national levels with Ivoirian social barometers indicating that people were not really content as yet with social justice, political, and other fundamental arrangements (Doyle 2011; Amnesty International 2011).

The Problem of Inflexibility

The second evidence of increased divisiveness was manifested in Gbagbo's and Ouattara's inflexibility. Both presidents were inflexible in terms of their individual perceptions of the role of governance and the use of political power. Even though Ouattara's economic measures were unpopular in the past (Konaté 2005), he had waited since 1990–1993 (when he served as prime minister) to assume power, and he was not going to capitulate to Gbagbo. As prime minister, he actually ran the country for about a year while President Houphouët-Boigny was ill. After Houphouët-Boigny's death in 1993, Ouattara assumed that he would naturally keep the country going until elections were called. Unfortunately, Bédié, head of parliament and knowing the time would come, had carefully manipulated the constitution some years back to position himself as heir. With Article 11 of the national constitution, Bédié took power and placed himself as interim president (Konaté 2005). Now declared winner of the 2010 elections, Ouattara's time had come and no compromises were going to be entertained.

The inflexibility of the two presidents reached fever pitch when ECOWAS asked Gbagbo to step down and he refused (Butty 2011). Ouattara also pointedly refused to go away or negotiate with Gbagbo. He did not see why he needed to negotiate with Gbagbo, whom he most probably viewed as a criminal who had violated the rules of democracy and civil society, created all kinds of impossible conditions for Ivoirians, and forcefully sought to usurp the presidency by dictatorial force. Though Ouattara's inflexibility had contributed to fear and uncertainty, he probably had his eyes on restorative and transformative justice for the North and all other Ivoirians who had been disenfranchised by Ivoirité and other forms of exclusion and oppressive economic and political legacies and programs.

Other important elements also sustained Ouattara's inflexibility. In 1990 when Houphouët-Boigny brought him in from the BCEAO to rescue the Ivoirian economy, he understood what needed to happen. And having served in the IMF, transforming his nation's economic condition was much more significant in a scenario where a country that was once so successful had collapsed to the status of a fragile state. Even nations that could not compete with the Ivoirian economy when it was at its economic glory were now part of the ECOWAS and AU telling Côte d'Ivoire what to do. With a PhD in economics, and with extensive service in highly rated and advanced international monetary systems, Ouattara's confidence, which increased his inflexibility, positioned him as the president who can turn things around and transform the nation.

Gbagbo and his cronies, who were used to enjoying political elite privileges, and who were not sure which direction things would go in a Ouattara presidency, became frightened and adopted an inflexible posture. Gbagbo moved to nullify the elections in six or so regions, and with the help of the CCIC declared himself the winner of the presidency. Gbagbo's inflexibility intensified because of his addiction to autocracy and power. He was not trying to get others to collaborate with him on a broader vision of sustaining a democratic Côte d'Ivoire. He wanted to impose himself on Ivoirians as a liberator of the nation from Houphouët-Boigny, who was addicted to France. In much of Africa, the liberator does not ever want to leave, and the case of Zimbabwe highlights this view (Godwin 2011).

In addition, Gbagbo's inflexibility was not going to give Ouattara the space to practice his northern Islamic politics. Strangely, Gbagbo saw Côte d'Ivoire as belonging to the southerners, to Christians (but this is a colonial religion), and to the Akans and the Kru, and he was going to stay to protect all of these arrangements. Thus, the two dimensions of inflexibility translate into a fight between two massive giants, which in turn wrought social chaos (disarray, confusion, uncertainty, fear, disruptions, and violence) on Ivoirians (United Nations Security Council 2011b).

The point here is that when powerful political elites fight and adopt inflexibility as the only conflict approach in a fragile nation where the population relies on the government for almost everything, suffering and social chaos are accentuated. While Gbagbo tried to get access to revenue by cutting an oil deal with a Russian company (Smith 2011), Ouattara tried to sabotage him by shutting down monetary access, but that action led to the stoppage of payment to civil servants, as well as resources for the continuation of some crucial services. The adverse economic instability that followed was absorbed by private enterprises because they were either too greedy to help or were not strong and large enough to sustain the nation while top leaders viciously fought with each other.

The inflexibility of the two presidents led to shortages in cash, food, water, electricity, and health services, and brought the international community (the UN, the AU, EU, the United States, and NGOs) back into Ivoirian internal affairs. NGOs picked up the pieces of broken, hungry, ill, and displaced citizens, supported refugees, and helped with other basic necessities and shortages. The ethnic, political, and social animosity built up prior to the presidential conflict (Skogseth 2006) increased during the conflict. Many children were separated from their parents and suffered psychological trauma

(Palitza 2012). The specific support for patients with HIV/AIDS, already a highly infectious disease in West Africa (USAID 2012; Chirot 2006) simply slowed in some places. Some Ivoirians with dual citizenship fled to Europe and other nations, and many others painfully moved to neighboring countries as refugees. During the presidential conflict, Côte d'Ivoire, a tropical beauty, with Abidjan serving as the party capital of Africa (welcoming visitors from other African nations and Europe), finally disintegrated into political chaos.

The Problem of Corruption

The third evidence showed up in the corruption that occurred during the presidential conflict. Top political elites were aware that things had broken down and that business as usual was not going to be the case anymore. Because Western nations decided that Gbagbo was the culprit and declared his regime persona non grata in the EU and the United States, they had to find ways to solve their problems. Gbagbo and his cronies also recognized that Ouattara is a change agent, an austerity advocate who thrives on economic transparency. While holding on to their inflexible posture, they also embarked on looting of the national treasury (Smith 2011). The looting of the treasury translated into economic problems, which in turn hurt the nation, especially the lower stratum, by removing monies from circulation, payrolls, and services and diverting them to secret accounts (Smith 2011).

Ironically, even though Gbagbo's corrupt and inflexible autocratic governance behavior was obvious, he was offered asylum by the United States, and Boston University offered him a teaching position. Clearly, faculty salary at Boston University was never going to match the economic privileges he enjoyed as president in a nation where he had so much advantage in terms of power and control. But why did the United States and Boston University want a dictator? The reason may be found in Chomsky's (2011) argument which implicates the United States as a nation that discounts true democracy and prefers autocratic dictatorship in many nations. Whereas Ivoirians decried elite political corruption in their nation, a super-powerful nation, the United States, was willing to reward Gbagbo, the architect of their misery.

If Gbagbo had accepted the offer and moved to Boston, then he may have brought along some key members of his team, and they would not have arrived empty-handed. In addition, he may have been able to circulate himself around so many other elite universities and fora, teaching his version of crude political governance, and giving Westerners, at least those bent on discounting Africa nations, more ammunition to hurt them. It is a good thing that he never took the offer, especially now that investigations have found him to be a criminal in The Hague's International Criminal Court (ICC). The criminal charges by the international court highlight the questionable wisdom of the United States' and Boston University's decision to invite him to asylum.

The Problem of Violence

The fourth evidence came from the rampant violence during the presidential conflict. When violence occurs in a fragile nation, its deepest impact is felt in the poorer population. Violence during the presidential conflict and after the conflict led to social chaos, fear, and insecurity (Amnesty International 2011). Violence also disconnected people from access to health services, food, water, and electricity. In this scenario a violence loop developed. With food and water shortages, people engaged in desperate actions (looting, vandalism, and infrastructural destruction) which looped back to violence. When people are involved in acts of violence, they often do not care who is affected.

The evidence of violence, much of which amounted to crime, led to the imposition of sanctions on Gbagbo and his regime by the UN Security Council Resolution 1975 on March 30, 2011. The unanimous fifteen-member vote in the Security Council imposed sanctions, travel bans, and asset freezes, and authorized UNOCI troops to protect civilians who were being targeted by Gbagbo forces (United Nations Security Council Resolution 1975). The security resolution follows ECOWAS' call for an international intervention force. Moreover, the sheer number of people killed (about three thousand) and those displaced (about a million people) (Sekularac, 2011), points to the extreme adverse impact of the conflict. Sustaining his intense culpability in dealing in violence and abuses, the International Criminal Court charged Gbagbo with the responsibility for co-perpetrating four crimes—murder, rape and other forms of sexual violence, persecution, and inhuman acts (International Criminal Court 2011).

The nature of the various levels of violence (intimidation, psychological warfare, property destruction, and looting) during the presidential conflict caused important national activities/projects to be put on hold. Education (school attendance) in the context of fear ceased or became sporadic (Dean 2011) as young people were uncertain about security conditions. The disruption of education slows the nation down in terms of social development. This is because skills acquired from educational activities sets the next generation up for creativity and national transformation. As well, the health sector, infrastructural projects, and other important national development activities were slowed or halted because of the fear imposed by violence. Disrupting the health sector slows down the national efforts to deal with tropical and other diseases such as leprosy—770 cases were detected in 2011 (IRIN 2012)—and HIV/AIDS (USAID 2012).

The tragic consequence of violence is that it shuts down so many options. It is also linked to the destruction of human resources, workplaces, and systems. When workplace systems are vandalized, once stability occurs, the government often starts programs and their documentation all over again. This destructive cycle occurs mostly in fragile nations where new regimes often have to start from scratch. Starting over and over again leads to delays in economic and social developments. Close to a million people fled their homes during post-election violence (Bally 2011). This means that many or all displaced Ivoirians, including children, lived in very desolate conditions.

Finally, discussions regarding restarting Côte d'Ivoire's economy had post-conflict violence in mind. Jump-starting the economy was going to be slow and painful. The issue of unpaid salaries for previous and continuing work during the conflict also point to the nature of the conflict as having heavily affected the labor sector. Export trade ground to a halt. About 400,000 tons of cocoa beans languished at Ivoirian ports. Cocoa is the backbone of Ivoirian national revenue. When Ouattara mentions that he will pacify the country in one or two months, it was clear that post-conflict violence was still presenting difficult challenges (Côte d'Ivoire: Gbagbo Surrenders 2011).

The World Bank and the International Monetary Fund (IMF) entered the scene with promises of monetary assistance. These two systems have been linked to the tragic conditions of many African nations, and to see them getting involved in Côte d'Ivoire intending to partner with Africa Development Bank (ADB) invokes concerns about their intentions. Nonetheless, the systems were involved because Ouattara, the new leader, allowed them access to Ivoirian affairs. The World Bank and IMF have generally been categorized as extremely dangerous systems to poor and fragile nations. After more than three decades of external interventions, the partnership with external monetary systems has generally offered benefits to political elites. Not many substantive benefits have reached the lower strata of Côte d'Ivoire and other African nations. Senegal, a close neighbor to Côte d'Ivoire, was visited by the IMF and was forced to devalue its currency and adopt some insane adjustments. The devastation that followed is criminal and heartbreaking (Moyers 2003).

Chapter Seven

Vapid Insatiability Theory

This book explored the presidential conflict between Presidents Gbagbo and Ouattara in view of teasing out useful and/or adverse implications of the conflict on Côte d'Ivoire, and to some extent on the West African region and beyond. This chapter begins by examining two critical concepts, democracy and democratic capitalism, specifically in the light of governance and civil society in Côte d'Ivoire. Then, it presents a new theory—the vapid insatiability theory—as a way to view the presidential conflict in Côte d'Ivoire and perhaps other similar conflicts.

DEMOCRACY OR DEMOCRATIC CAPITALISM

Democracy has become a buzzword used by political elites across the globe. It is used in the place of outright public violence to enforce fear, conformity, and social order. Unfortunately, enforced social order always breeds all kinds of social conflict. Deceivingly, once trapped in the grid of enforced social order, many societies, specifically ones in the Western world, appear organized and tranquil to insiders who do not care to look further and to outsiders. However, such social order is the result of carefully constructed political, economic, and social controls which have replaced the actual pursuit of democracy or its ideals with "democratic capitalism"—a system preoccupied with self-serving and emotive uses of power.

This is to say that the current global social order is more rapidly promising multiple future states of chaos (see Stiglitz 2002 on the impact of globalization; Bond 2006; Sewpaul and Hölscher 2004 on neo-liberal capitalism), than it is of global collaboration, justice, and collective responsibility. Alexis de Tocqueville (2000), who struggled with the notion of democracy as something socially useful in society, has mostly been relegated to the past as irrelevant in the new scheme of hyper- neo-liberal capitalist pursuits (democratic capitalism) where corporate control of policies, as well as economic, political, and social activities worldwide, have redefined democratic interactions in terms of the power of capital (see Chomsky 2016).

At one time, the pursuit of democracy was perhaps a serious and meaningful endeavor, but that was at a time when people were not so affluent and apathetic to each other. Also, that was the time when there was some semblance of positive conscience, and also a time when emphasis was placed on human dignity rather than privileges derived from economic power. Moreover, democracy was meaningful at a time when people were not polarized and functionally divisive because of economic, political, race, ethnic, class, gender, and power differentiation dynamics.

In the early 1940s through the 1960s in Côte d'Ivoire, democracy was a goal worthy of pursuit. It is still worthy of pursuit because many of the nation's remote towns and villages desire all kinds of transformations that would give them a taste of liberty with which to construct some sense of self-determination. But beginning with Houphouët-Boigny through to Gbagbo, the content of democracy was dramatically altered. It was often used in political campaigns, but the ultimate goal was the construction of autocratic dictatorship to generate interminable benefits funneled to the powerful ruling elites. Despite its radical alteration, Ivoirians conformed to follow Houphouët-Boigny and successive leaders, religiously believing and clinging to democracy's efficacious and liberatory magic.

But there is yet another dimension to the altered nature of democracy. What powerful nations define under the rubrics of international democratic engagement is a collection of economic and political interests designed to expropriate resources from resource-rich fragile nations. When poor nations lack useful raw materials with which to bargain with powerful Western nations for their survival, interactions about democracy or "mutual interests" are generally mute. The tragic silence during the Rwandan genocide (1994) serves as an excellent example here, and Côte d'Ivoire is only lucky to still be in play because it has cocoa and coffee with which to bargain for its existence.

However, within Western nations, democracy has largely been reconfigured and anchors the rapid dissemination of fears and insecurities. Arrogant pontification of self-inflation drives an immutable wedge between the search for liberatory truth (resources) about who people are as citizens and what they can become as human beings. In the end, the idea of democracy is no longer owned by the people. It is no longer an ideal that can be fired up and used to chart positive directions focused on collective social coherence, stopping every now and then to make corrections when things go off course. Instead, the new form of democracy (democratic capitalism) is owned and policed by the super-powerful elite, and like other common commodities, it is peddled and sold with conditions on the global market. This is the kind of democracy that landed in Côte d'Ivoire in the 1960s, and was peddled by successive political elites from Houphouët-Boigny to Bédié through to Gbagbo.

Who are the owners of democratic capitalism? These are powerful global individuals, mostly unknown, and also mostly hidden behind their massive capital-generating systems. They masquerade as the "good guys" and convince populations to trust them. They are eerily "fraternally" connected to powerful elites in poor nations, and it was in this regard that President Houphouët-Boigny entrusted Côte d'Ivoire to France, its colonial nemesis. No matter where democratic capitalism surfaces, and even when it is obvious that it has contributed to the violation of human rights and dignity, its proponents insist that it is the only path toward true democracy, justice, rights, and fairness.

As "democratic capitalism" is peddled as the preferred gateway to success, many fragile nations also become its defender. In Côte d'Ivoire, most citizens unwittingly participate in democratic capitalism, assuming that this is democracy. For many Ivoirians, democracy has many positive manifestations and is still viewed as the most promising ideal with which to manage not only human aspirations, conflict, and risks, but also social justice in ways they hope would create benefits for everyone.

In struggling with the extreme polarizations in society, often caused by the absence of or diminishing democratic ideals, Rawls pointed out that all social primary goods are to be continuously shared based on the principle of equal opportunity for all (Rawls 1971). However, because of the arrogance of death-wielding democratic capitalist proponents in his time, Rawls insisted that an unequal distribution may occur only when that inequality is to the advantage of the disadvantaged.

In a realistic democratic pursuit, Rawls's argument is practicable. But within democratic capitalism, Rawls's position is not only problematic but is also considered dangerous and socially divisive by powerful ruling elites. They would argue that Rawls's principle is contrary to the pursuit of liberal democratic capitalism, and that in order to maintain social and economic coherence, such equal-opportunity talk must be eliminated from all societies. Complementing Rawls's efforts on justice for all, Noam Chomsky's *Requiem for the American Dream* (2017) offers the dismal ways in which democracy and self-determination have been fragmented in the United States. However, this fragmentation of democracy has global implication. Gbagbo's actions showed this to be true in Côte d'Ivoire as he sought to eliminate all opposition or any attempt to think about distributive justice. Of course, what makes democratic capitalism popular among the ruling elites in poor nations is that it empowers a social intercourse that is highly subjective. It in no uncertain terms makes economic success an essential element of elite political power and privileges religiously guarded to ensure subjective benefits at the expense of citizens.

In wealthy advanced nations, insisting on democratic ideals exposes competing emotivisms which have primed citizens to admire only those who are able to associate democracy with affluence, hence democratic capitalism. Those rational positions, which are less skillfully argued in terms of ensuring that actual democracy remains an ideal relevant for collective social coherence, often collapse under the weight of extremely powerful and privileged democratic capitalist impositions.

This is because the proponents of democratic capitalism wield super power, have hyper-influence, and control access to almost all contextual and/or global resources. In addition, even though responsible discourses on democracy, good governance, and justice continue to reach the public, extremely powerful democratic capitalist proponents continue to successfully dampen, if not drown, their impact. They militarize young people, militarize police forces across the globe, make the arms race attractive, turn people internally and externally against each other, and create massive addictions through flooding the public with goods that titillate their appetites yet simultaneously force them to become indefinite and mindless consumers who turn against each other for any reason.

The consequences of redefining democracy into democratic capitalism include the abandonment of care and social responsibility. What follows are massive social confusion, conflict, suffering, social apathy, and socio-economic and socio-political paralysis. If most citizens are essentially unable to challenge governments in advanced nations without tragic consequences, then Gbagbo may have simply reasoned and concluded that the level of citizen mediocrity in Côte d'Ivoire guaranteed that he could do as he pleased.

Consequently, in Côte d'Ivoire, the redefinition of democracy into "democratic dictatorship" created a mostly conformist context infused with fear and socially immobilized but angry citizens. The idea that democracy was hijacked and turned into a dictatorship (Houphouët-Boigny from 1960 to 1993, and Bédié, Guéï, and Gbagbo from 1993 to 2010) in Côte d'Ivoire was not surprising. What was surprising was the overt way it was done. The end result was the massive social conflict and misery that destabilized the nation as Ivoirians consistently returned for more punishment every time promises of democracy were dangled before them by the same powerful elite bent on destroying them.

Ironically, when the people finally awoke to enact a "democratic" revolution, they only had violence as conflict resolution tools (coups, military actions, vandalism, looting, and more violence). Unfortunately, conflict resolution which defaults to violence increases political apathy, social agony, and misery. This was clearly the case in Côte d'Ivoire, especially with regard to the actions of presidents Gbagbo and Ouattara. In a way, the Ivoirian political elite before, during, and after the presidential conflict created a totalitarian asylum which they continued to misname as democracy.

Conflict, Democracy, and Peace

Because the notion of power and the idea of democracy were being thrown around without much action to sustain them in Côte d'Ivoire, African and international bodies (AU, ECOWAS, and the UN) had to change tack, especially in their effort to sustain some measure of democracy. In the 1990s the region of West Africa was besieged with conflicts. The response to the conflict was ECOWAS's regional military force, the ECOMOG. ECOMOG was vital in Liberia and Sierra Leone. Although there were difficult logistical challenges with the ECOMOG, its use supplied vital lessons which ECOWAS used in their response to the Côte D'Ivoire scenario (Arthur 2010). Primary among these lessons was learning to sustain an impartial posture against dictatorship which they saw was advantageous to conflict resolution, democracy, and peace.

Similarly, the international community and the UN Security Council changed their approach by taking a stand against autocratic behaviors. The UN Security Council authorized the use of force (Côte d'Ivoire and Libya), while regional and international organizations (AU, ECOWAS, and NATO) increased their profiles as determined security-providing global players (Bellamy and Williams 2011).

The process of democracy in Côte d'Ivoire was something positive with future benefits (Fauré 1993). This was the period when Gbagbo challenged Houphouët-Boigny and multi-party elections were allowed. Even though Houphouët-Boigny and his PDCI leadership found ways in 1990 to ensure their continued dominance, leadership in Africa required the kind of transformation that would sustain democracy, economic capabilities, and self-determination (Ismail 2008; Klaas 2008).

Unfortunately, dealing with violence has become a new "elite-making" process which negatively impacts peace agreements. Those who gain elite status through conflict and violence view the pursuit of peace as a disabling mechanism to the pipeline of benefits. As well, peace-making and power sharing devised in peace accords only benefit the top political entities. They lack linkages between the top and the larger citizenry in terms of actual participation (Ismail 2008). This is perhaps the more challenging problem when international groups are involved in negotiations to generate peace-accord processes that are often not designed for the benefit of members of entire nations.

In addition, there is a link between horizontal inequalities and the emergence of violent conflict. The horizontal inequalities found at the elite level and socio-economic horizontal inequality found at the common citizenry levels are catalysts for violent conflict. As for the political elite, being excluded horizontally can lead to mobilization of supporters (Brown and Langer 2010). This was clearly the case with Gbagbo before 2000, and Ouattara in his contention with Gbagbo in 2010/2011. Horizontal inequality also propels the common citizenry to take sides, often choosing the political elites they perceive will better sustain their survival. This link was evident in the inequalities created by the doctrine of Ivoirité which was deranging enough to cause a civil war in the 2002 (Kouadio 2009).

Moreover, the civil conflict in Côte d'Ivoire is also linked to citizenship concerns. Several groups, especially the international ones, were unsuccessful in helping broker peace because they did not take the Ivoirité-citizenship issue seriously. It was the internal resolution devised by Ivoirians that appeared to work as long as they understood that Ivoirité and citizenship concern were the source of conflict. In 2007, Gbagbo agreed to share power with the rebel leader Guillame Soro, who was made prime minister (Bah 2010).

However, there were other disruptive elements which made democracy uncertain and the presidential conflict inevitable. The "Young Patriots" were an important and powerful element in Côte d'Ivoire. Started in 2002 as a consistent pool of Gbagbo supporters, their claim was to finally, in a sort of second attempt, liberate Côte d'Ivoire from France. Their posture was clearly a leaf from Gbagbo's anti-colonial/neo-colonial philosophy. Intermingled with their political liberation agenda was their quest for representation and affirmation in a social context that was both confusing and divided by political strife, social-justice deprivation, and ethnic tension wrought by Ivoirité (Banégas 2006). Even though they were important within Gbagbo's political configuration, they were nonetheless a volatile bunch (following the violent leader; see Blé Goudé 2006) that made democracy and civil society impossible through intimidation and violence from their inception in 2002 until 2011 (Quist-Arcton 2011).

The picture of Côte d'Ivoire is one of glory in the 1960s and 1970s and then of gradual decay in the 1980s. Many factors led to the disintegration, for instance, the increased surplus of cocoa on the global market, the stoking of ethnic differentiation through the introduction of Ivoirité, and general political and social deprivations. The civil war was the result of inequalities generated by several circumstances, including political impropriety and ethnic difference (Chirot 2006; Collett 2006).

Nestled within the difficult consideration of the presidential conflict and its implications are several other crucial issues, such as land (for instance, indigenous versus migrant ownership) and the ethnic dynamics involved with it. Land has been a source of conflict in the Southwest region of Côte d'Ivoire, where many of the cocoa farms are sustained by a high volume of immigrant labor (Colin, Kouamé, and Soro 2007). In addition, the lack of good transportation to school was already an issue before the presidential conflict. But during the conflict, many children were slotted into child labor, consequently disrupting their education. Child labor was connected to subsidizing family revenue and survival by involving children in labor (Canagarajah and Nielsen 2001).

In Côte d'Ivoire, as anywhere else, children of the elite live spoiled and privileged lives, paying no heed or regard to the majority of the lower-stratum children whose parents must, on a daily basis, scrounge their livelihood together to sustain their poor families. It is when this excruciating option emerges that parents trump schooling and default their children to labor as a way to enhance what little revenue comes in. It would make sense that land issues, specifically ownership rights, and all children's right to education would need to form part of any future democratic and peaceful transformation in Côte d'Ivoire.

Vapid Insatiability Theory

The presidential conflict created the space for the construction of a new theoretical option that is slightly more critical than the theories (elite, intergroup conflict theory, critical feminist, internal corruption, and postmodernism) discussed in a previous chapter. This new theory is much more critical in the way it delineates the implications of the presidential conflict and the factors that underlie the behavior and actions of the two presidents.

The theory delineates two relatable variables by explaining the relationship of the variables in terms of a given problem (see Shoemaker, Tankard, and Lasorsa 2004). The more exciting part of the theory is its use not only to explain the presidential conflict but also to create the possibilities of responding to the question "Then what?" with creative and responsible interactive prescriptions.

Theory's Background

The presence of massive global changes has introduced thriving civil societies, some gender equity, and some levels of human rights to several parts of the world, but so many social contexts are still caught up in inflexible socio-political, socio-economic, and socio-religious discomfort. The nature of the negative uses of political power (dictatorship, military repressions, and totalitarian regimes) continues to manifest as a critical global challenge. The conflict between presidents Gbagbo and Ouattara clearly demonstrates that citizens of fragile nations have major work to do in terms of transforming the behavior of those who seek to govern.

From examining the presidential conflict and its implications in Côte d'Ivoire, it became clear that Ivoirians were locked in a struggle between citizens battling for survival and political elites who were never satisfied with having much more than enough. The nature of never being satisfied with much more than enough is well demonstrated when considering the credit default swap market. This is a secretly managed monetary system by hedge fund practitioners. In 2008, the United States' treasury market was about 4.5 trillion dollars, and the United States stock market was about 22 trillion dollars, but the credit default swap market (which is hidden from regular open banking activities) was 45 trillion dollars (Moon 2008).

The point here is that extremely powerful elite individuals with hyper-economic appetites are never satisfied even with the accumulation of trillions of dollars. Forty-five trillion dollars in 2008 is the result of unregulated banking activities, much of which is at the expense of less advantaged global citizens. The idea of "too much is not enough" is applicable to political power, authority, control, wealth, and much more. The phenomenon of not being satisfied with having too much was exemplified in President Gbagbo after he manipulated to extend his years in the Ivorian presidency from 2000 to 2010. Even after losing the elections in 2010, he refused to leave office. This behavior and phenomenon is known as vapid insatiability, and extends beyond the Ivoirian context. The rage to have much more than too much has become a normalized socio-political and socio-economic dynamic in many parts of the globe.

In more detail, the vapid insatiability theory explains the inverse relationships between social groups, for instance, relationships of power, governance, wealth, and dominance. To illustrate the theory, consider the relationship between superiors (administrators) who determine the course of events, and subordinates who must comply with these decisions or face dire consequences. Conversely, most positive actions coming from subordinates in view of self-determination or rectification of inequalities are often met with dehumanizing inverse actions from the top.

However, within all relationships there are fluctuating dynamics that point in several directions. But in vapid insatiability relationships, there is an upward and downward impact. As for powerful elite, upward impact = benefits, and the downward impact = production of misery or disadvantages for the lower stratum. On the part of the lower stratum, any action demanding rights and dignity directed upward toward the powerful elite usually results in a downward draft of anger which produces more harm to their already weakened existence.

Thus, for the lower stratum, upward impact = more misery, and downward impact = misery and violence. The misery and violence in the lower stratum is also augmented because of poor-on-poor abuses and harms sustained by political and other elites through various polarization processes. For instance, much of the apathy, greed, anger, antagonism, and powerlessness visible in the lower stratum of Côte d'Ivoire were linked to people's basic desire for self-determination and material sufficiency. Within such desperation, actions for survival and the struggle for scarce resources led to violence, which resulted in devastating consequences to the poor (consider black-on-black violence in the United States, or lower-stratum soldiers and guerrillas raping already vulnerable women in many conflict contexts of the globe).

When insatiability is occurring on the part of the upper stratum, automatically scarcity, social limitations, and unprecedented struggle and violence eventuate at the lower bottom. While limitations and shortages are increasing at the lower stratum, insatiable access increases at the upper stratum as the political elite with their extreme power do everything to sustain greed, apathy, and antagonism against the lower stratum, or anyone for that matter, who tries to destabilize their carefully constructed context of insatiable privileges. The continuity of such hyper-privilege also requires a unique kind of power generally found among dictator presidents. Such power allows them total control of the nation's revenue, resources, labor, remunerations, rights, and privileges.

Thus, insatiability is linked to a state of perpetual dissatisfaction which insists that too much is not enough. Insatiability is much like the concept of eternal colonialism (Benjamin and Hall 2010) where the raging drive (much beyond the desire to own something for satisfaction) to accumulate unprecedented power, wealth, assets, and resources, and to stake ownership of material and immaterial resources, leads to the desire to enact an eternal control. Such insatiable power guarantees for all times the continued control of all resources, benefits, and privileges at the expense of citizens in a context and beyond. But while insatiable control is occurring, the populations from whose contexts resources are drawn remain defaulted to lives of subservience, underdevelopment, instability, and perpetual dependency.

The vapid insatiability theory holds that the actions causing dire consequences between groups (privilege on the one hand, and adversity on the other) are understandable within the grid of socially constructed inverse relationships that yields perpetual benefits to the powerful and/or the dominant party, and misery and disadvantages to the subordinated. Actions against those trapped in the disadvantaged inverse grid are continuously brutal, vicious, and uncompromising. These actions never have regard for people in terms of respecting rights, dignity, and self-determination. The actions reveal various levels of pleasure derived from human suffering so that the more suffering there is, the more misery is heaped on disadvantaged populations. In Côte d'Ivoire, the feuding presidents used force and violence indiscriminately to achieve their whims, but the power of their force was concentrated on punishing the lower stratum.

Furthermore, even though the actions (often demanding rights and privileges) of the lower stratum directed at the upper stratum are less antagonistic, pleading, and conciliatory, the inverse reaction from the upper stratum is always devastating. In other words, weakened and often humbled posturing from the lower stratum is a signal for the upper stratum to increase its strength and temerity by heaping more misery on the lower stratum. A fair test to determine whether or not to use vapid insatiability theory to evaluate a conflict scenario is to find characteristics and actions which portend positive (for the dominant) and negative (for the weaker) consequences being demonstrated in an insatiable unidirectional trajectory.

Testing the Theory

Insatiable accumulation of power, resources, or wealth comes from the invincibility that empowers individuals to demand absolute ownership and control of "good life" and "high privileges" while shunning bad experiences. Coupled with this drive is the desire to exercise absolute control at all times. As with all insatiable hyper-accumulation, bad consequences exist, and they are often defaulted to enemies or in the case of Côte d'Ivoire, to the poor and lower stratum of society.

The vapid insatiability theory points out that insatiable hyper-accumulation generally results in the total abandonment of reason. In this scenario dignity and rights are trumped in favor of the insatiable pursuits that harm people. During the presidential conflict in Côte d'Ivoire, scarcity of food and the lack of provisional resources increased. Generally, those at the lower stratum were severely harmed. Conversely, it is doubtful that the two presidents, the privileged upper class, and many of the elite middle upper strata went to bed hungry. These privileged social strata were closest to the control of national income and resources. Vapid insatiability insists that the link between the upper stratum or dominant group and the lower stratum or weaker group is always extremely high so that social control and the measures of misery dumped on the weaker realm are decisively targeted. This was precisely the case in Côte d'Ivoire. The presidents knew exactly where each other's constituents were at all times, and each responded with calculated brutal measures to weaken each side.

Through the vapid insatiability theory, it becomes easier to see how in conflict scenarios similar to the Ivoirian presidential conflict, the group that helps the upper stratum lock down the lower stratum in perpetual misery is often an insatiable middle stratum. The middle stratum exists to create a buffer zone between the upper class and the lower class. This group is generally assured of material rewards and promises of advancement if it does well in its efforts to keep the lower-stratum "riff raff" under control. In protecting its own privileges, the middle stratum accepts injunctions from the upper stratum to propagate all kinds of systemic and structural violence. It replicates negation, exclusion, and abandonment using tightly guarded perspectives (academics), processes and rules (law enforcement and courts), and business models (managers). All of these actions mostly protect the upper stratum, but drain dignity, rights, privileges, and life out of the population in the lower stratum.

The Ivoirian presidential conflict clearly demonstrates this typology. The presidents protected themselves by using the services of the middle stratum (military, civil servants, judges, and other government workers), who in turn punished the lower stratum through all kinds of deprivations (shortage of payment for work service, food shortages, water and electricity shortages, and much more). The point here is that insatiable hyper-accumulation's logic is to disregard people's desperate conditions. This was evident in Côte d'Ivoire, where insatiable hyper-accumulation of power and its use trended negatively in two directions, one toward innumerable harms (human-rights abuse, political unrest, and civil uncertainty), and the other toward the total disregard of distributive justice (scarcity, increased disadvantages, and economic and social misery).

Vapid insatiability theory also points out that insatiability is also present in the lower stratum of society. The level of such insatiability has graver consequences. Instability in the lower stratum drives out options for creativity, meaningfulness, ownership, and constructive power, while entrenching rage, dependency, and vapid consumerism. This is the signal that vapidity and insatiability have converged. The upper stratum accumulates and consumes life and meaning out of the lower stratum, and the lower stratum simply collapses and succumbs to vapid consumerism.

However, the perspective that poor folks are vapid consumers is interesting. In their case, consumption here is defined as a dependency that shuts out production, creativity, and self-reliance. The poor of Côte d'Ivoire appear to be completely dependent on the economic decisions of the upper political leaders, whose sense of privilege is defined around their desires and tastes of what is economically good or bad. The irony of dependence on such vapid relationships is that the elite have no direct interest in lifting everyone up to a level of shared knowledge and privileges. This phenomenon of inverse adverse relationship between dominant and weaker groups goes back to Galtung (1971) who gave it a global spin. Simply, the cozy relationship dominant nations have with each other is derived from, but simultaneously adversarial to, weaker nations.

An interesting dimension considered by vapid insatiability theory is that in the inverse adversarial scenario, most people are aware that they are being exploited and dehumanized, but many of them resign themselves to powerlessness because they believe that no amount of revolution or interdiction is going to introduce actual democracy, justice, or fairness. Succumbing to powerlessness is based on the simple argument that those who rise up and create revolutions eventually become oppressors and dictators in the future, and so on. President Gbagbo was clearly a shining example of this conclusion. It follows then that the more the powerful or the dominant accumulate power, the more dissatisfied they are. The adversarial inverse of their dissatisfaction leads to the increased stagnation of those at the bottom, depriving them of progress and self-determination. Ironically, even when the disadvantaged stratum is aware of the problem and knows what to do to enact liberation, most citizens choose instead to depend on the depriving actors for everything. This means that no matter the sophistication of liberation activism, insatiable political elites (autocrats, dictators, etc.) guarantee themselves unequivocal protection and benefits designed into their adversarial inverse relationship with the subordinated.

For instance, the activist revolutions in Tunisia, Egypt, and Libya did not change the relationship between men and women. In these nations, men still wield political power and control governance while women languish at the bottom. To explain this phenomenon, vapid insatiability views the North African revolutions as a scheme that overthrew men and re-entrenched another set of them in a configuration that deifies masculinity as the insatiable heir to the governance, political, and social systems.

Thus, vapid insatiability defines the adversarial inverse condition wherein masculine over feminine, rich over poor, and deserving over undeserving relationships deny or delay actual democracy, equal opportunity, and self-determination. Back in Côte d'Ivoire, even though President Ouattara finally assumed power, his post-conflict model of political governance has tactically empowered the same old political elite who support his agenda. For Ouattara to escape the analysis of vapid instability, his governance approach must go beyond business as usual (working on the economy and empowering men), to include women in high offices (the vice presidential position). This move guarantees that women may someday achieve the presidency. He would also need to include newcomers who have generally been spectators as elites from previous generations swallowed up power and opportunities.

To conclude the presentation of the theory it is useful to clarify that "vapid" and "insatiability" were deliberately linked to denote totalistic emptiness and aimlessness. "Having too much" and "never satisfied" denotes a heightened level of indomitable human greed which severs connection to people and deifies exploitation and totalitarian accumulation. The coup de grâce is evident in what vapid insatiability theory describes as a carefully and psychologically engineered negation and infighting inserted into the bottom stratum so that people are never able to rise beyond their decrepit conditions. This means that even when the bottom populations try to work things out in ways that would benefit them without antagonizing the middle and upper strata, they are never allowed to exit from misery. Each time they try, an active adversarial inverse action leaps out to thwart their efforts.

Theory Applied to the Presidential Conflict

This theory has tremendous implication for the Ivoirian scenario. When political and other elite members of Côte d'Ivoire speak of the idea of power, they are speaking about something that is far more advanced than the traditional notion of associating it to responsibility and service. "Being powerful" in Côte d'Ivoire means that you have adopted a triadic (colonial, neo-colonial, and distinctively Ivoirian autocratic) approach and stance. The negative use of political power affects socio-economic arrangements, where the powerful see themselves as distinct from the rest of the population. The idea of the upward and downward relationship sustained by the impact of power insatiability has tremendous influence on how people relate to each other in social contexts. In Côte d'Ivoire, the governing elite uses its insatiable power to deprive the rest of the nation (specifically the poor majority at the bottom stratum) of options for distributive justice.

The vapid insatiability theory suggests that the actions causing the adversarial inverse consequences to the bottom stratum have several characteristics. The actions from the elite must always be eternally brutal, vicious, and uncompromising, and should never have regard for people (or in some cases very little regard for people). Its most distinguishing characteristic is its reveling in human suffering and misery so that the more suffering there is, the more it pushes the buttons of insatiable accumulation driven by unbridled totalitarian greed. In the Ivoirian presidential conflict, several of these characteristics were clearly present. Brutality is evidenced by the behavior and actions of two presidents who were more interested in their political careers and their indefinite longevity in the presidential system than they were concerned about the people for whom the government exists.

In this sense, President Gbagbo's continued use of Bédié's Ivoirité, his empowerment of the Young Patriots, and his sanction of a clandestine militia all with the intention of generating harms to President Ouattara and his supporters was his way of sending a warning to all Ivoirians that he intended to entrench an indefinite autocratic dictatorship. In addition, his behavior sought to downgrade the people's self-determination and their quest for a democracy of fairness. In fairness, both Gbagbo and Ouattara adopted inflexible and uncompromising stances as they insatiably fought for power at the expense of the people of Côte d'Ivoire.

Conversely, actions from the bottom stratum causing the adversarial inverse reaction from the upper stratum have several characteristics. The actions from the bottom are often powerless and more compromising. When Houphouët-Boigny sat in power for three decades, there was not much of a challenge from Ivoirian citizens. To his credit, Gbagbo was the only individual who challenged him and failed in 1990. Whereas the acquiescence from citizens may be construed as respect for the benign dictator who was both liberator and Côte d'Ivoire's founding father, the reticence was detrimental to the future of civil society in Côte d'Ivoire. Cultivating a sense of respect can also socialize a sense of powerlessness into the population so that citizens default to respect more than they would to truth-telling and expression of concerns about a dictator's indefinite sojourn in the presidency.

Furthermore, in Côte d'Ivoire, much as in other parts of the world, anger and violence on the part of the lower stratum have been manipulated in such a way that they are no longer directed at the powerful or dominant systems. For instance, no Ivoirian citizen is ever going to go off to France and attack the French for their past and present activities in Côte d'Ivoire, and neither would the same citizens ever willfully attack their elite leaders without some other elite instigating it. Simply put, powerful political elites and government systems view themselves as immutable personalities who cannot be touched or affected by the violence or demands of the lower stratum.

Recently, Uganda's President Museveni (Vision Reporter 2012) opined that he has become a better leader because of his longevity in power (more than thirty years in power). His speech was perhaps indirectly encouraging other elite dictators to use his "new profound" vapid philosophy to stake their hold on political power. Vapid insatiability simply shows that no matter what the relationships are in systems of governance, interacting groups, or other forms of power, the nature of the double inverse action reaching upward-downward is always beneficial to the top and disempowering to the bottom. This was explicitly exemplified in the Ivoirian presidential conflict.

Chapter Eight

Adverse Impact

The presidential conflict had adverse socio-economic, socio-political, and psycho-cultural impact on Côte d'Ivoire and beyond. This chapter discusses the specific features that show the links between use of insatiable political power and the social consequences that followed.

CONSEQUENCES

Socio-political Arrangement

The first element emerges from the socio-political arrangement in Côte d'Ivoire designed around colonial, post-colonial, and contemporary experiences. Colonial history and experience imposed (on those socialized within it and thereafter) conditions that led to the specific conflict between presidents Gbagbo and Ouattara. The mixture of colonial, post-colonial, and contemporary dynamics created a complex socio-economic (inequalities, poverty, and glaring lack of social justice) and socio-political (disenfranchised groups, political elite power struggles, desire to maintain Côte d'Ivoire with subjective philosophies of governance) dynamics.

These dynamics vehemently clashed with each other, allowing high levels of apathy, distrust, and anger between Ivoirians. Also, the presidential conflict simply milked past divisive conditions and increased the polarization that became the new normal of the Ivoirian society after the death of Houphouët-Boigny in 1993. The presidential conflict was characterized by the inflexibility that came to define post-colonial conditions and interactions in Côte d'Ivoire and beyond.

It is useful to point out that Gbagbo and Ouattara in Côte d'Ivoire replicated the behavior of other West African political leaders. The popular approach of political leadership in West Africa always defaulted to divisive interethnic and socio-economic derangements (McCauley 2017). In the effort to patch things up and to sustain the privileges of being on top, political leaders continue to negate the lessons of their own histories, especially the rectification of grievances that come from social justice concerns and demands. As long as autocratic and dictatorial propensities are continually socialized into the psyche of most Ivoirians, distrust of governance, apathy on the part of Ivoirians, and continued socio-political divisiveness may exist for a long time.

Socio-economic Arrangement

Since Côte d'Ivoire's independence in 1960, socio-economic arrangements and conditions favored the elites in power and helped them extend their sojourn in government indefinitely. The nation's economic success between the 1960s and early 1980s points to tremendous privileges enjoyed by elite Ivoirians. Instead of using the revenue from the economic success for dynamic infrastructural and social justice response across the nation (urban and rural), the political elite quickly consolidated themselves in power. As they jostled for power, they turned on each other, while disregarding national development. The dissatisfaction with each other and the manifestation of insatiability for political power were not based on unconditional love to positively govern Côte d'Ivoire. Rather, they were based on sustaining and enhancing subjective advantages and privileges.

The popular parading of solutions for democracy, economic recovery, and national development by Ivoirian political elites was a disguise for a totalistic state control. As well, the political elite unflinchingly entrenched themselves on top of the food chain without substantive plans for the extensive improvement of economic and social conditions across the nation. Not surprisingly, the presidential conflict and the inflexibility between the two presidents simply increased economic and social stagnation. The coup in 2002, political demonstrations, the civil war, disruption of people's daily affairs, and the demarcation of the nation into two separate entities (North and South), and then the presidential conflict in 2010/2011 all pointed to economic and social instability. In each successive period, political elites paraded promises that were never fulfilled to rescue the nation from its downward spiral.

Disjunction between Elite and Citizens

There was a disconnection between the governing elite and the Ivoirian people. The link between the government and the people in terms of services, responsibilities, and expectations was weak, hence the agreement in much of the literature that change must occur if Côte d'Ivoire was going to get better. However, because it appeared that most Ivoirians pushed for conditions that no longer permitted indefinite sojourn and/or dictatorship in the presidency, the incumbent political elite fought back and increased the propensity for national instability.

This is a phenomenon that is common in West Africa and is linked to the corruptive dynamics that are rampant in political governance. The way the phenomenon manifests itself is simple. Political elites present themselves to citizens and make promises to deliver them from poverty, disease, and impossible social conditions. The promises are filled with empty titillations (better roads, adequate housing, sanitation infrastructure, electricity, good drinking water, improved healthcare, and so on). But as soon as the elections are over and political elites get into political office, their interaction with citizens ends. This disconnection was evident in Côte d'Ivoire. Rather than opt to responsibly use governance to serve the entire nation, much of the political elite's preoccupation was driven by emotive connections to ethnicity, nepotism, religion, allegiances, and subjective socio-economic and political interests. An added dimension of this disconnection was found in the number of active international groups, the UN and their various projects, NGOs, and other international efforts trying to bring basic services and relief to Ivoirians in cities, remote rural areas, and in refugee camps.

Political Uncertainty and Displacement

Political uncertainty in Côte d'Ivoire fueled increased migration with more than one million displaced Ivoirians (Sekularac 2011), who were afraid to return home (Amnesty International 2011). This particular phenomenon helps to additionally show the problem of increased social injustices. Civil war, coups, and power struggles among political elites in fragile nations always contribute to social and economic destabilization. For many citizens, specifically members of the lower stratum, migrating to safer places, no matter the hardship in those places, is a better option to violence.

However, migration was not just a phenomenon that occurred among the poor. Middle- and upper-class Ivoirians also sought exit to safer places. The difference between ending up in a refugee camp as displaced people or in the Western world lies in having skills (doctors, nurses, and other well-educated individuals). The migration of well-educated individuals ties into the mounting concern across Africa about the "brain drain" phenomenon (Yaqub 2007; Kaba 2004, 2005; Emeagwali 2003). Côte d'Ivoire, as well as other African nations, has lost specialized experts to Western labor establishments because migrating Ivoirians found much safer and more lucrative work outside conflict zones.

In addition, the report on militia groups forming bases in Liberia and coming back to terrorize Côte d'Ivoire (Shiner 2010) was akin to the migration scenario of the Hutus entering neighboring nations after the Rwandan genocide. Instead of many of them seeking productive work and relinquishing violence, they formed armed militia groups and continued to terrorize innocent civilians around border villages (Okosun and Kibiswa 2013). In Côte d'Ivoire, even after the conflict was over, the UN Security Council concluded in December 2011 that disgruntled Gbagbo supporters still clashed with armed civilians in Abidjan and the western part of the country (United Nations Security Council 2011a). Thus, the instability fomented by powerful political elites triggered negative consequences which included disconnection between governing elite and citizens, hate, rage, and violence.

Inappropriate Use of Political Power

The mandate of governance and political power is to serve and protect citizens. Unfortunately in Côte d'Ivoire, the negative use of governance and political power specifically affected political leaders' ability to encourage and support citizens' social-justice efforts. Instead of constructing encouraging rules to sustain justice and fairness activities for all citizens, the two presidents (for months) focused on subjective interests. Gbagbo focused on retaining the presidency and Ouattara focused on becoming the new Ivoirian leader. They disconnected from encouraging citizens to respect human rights and dignity and to structure themselves around conditions of social justice. Instead, the dominant actions were the encouragement of violent groups who clashed and negated each other across the country.

Moreover, before and during the presidential conflict, the lower stratum suffered various social injustices. Many Ivoirians had difficulties accessing common resources and opportunities and suffered displacement and violence. Newspapers, nongovernmental agencies, and United Nations personnel on the ground showed that human-rights abuses increased before, during, and after the presidential conflict (Amnesty International 2011). Another important reason that helps with understanding increases in social injustices is the Ivoirité program which successfully excluded the northern half of the country and/or anyone who did not fall into the characteristics of the program. Ivoirité was a divisive program set in place by Bédié in 1995. Citizens were also excluded from socio-economic benefits and many ended up migrating back to Burkina Faso, Mali, Guinea, or elsewhere.

Furthermore, Gbagbo tactically continued to use Ivoirité because it was advantageous to preclude oppositional Ivoirians from political participation. Gbagbo's clandestine use of the program leaped out when he lost elections in 2010 and refused to leave office. He did not want to leave the presidential office to someone he had all along believed had no real citizenship rights. If Ivoirité was a crucial reason for the civil war that erupted in 2002 (Kouadio 2009), then its revival and continued use in the 2010/2011 presidential conflict also helped to undermine human rights, dignity, and the quest for equal representation and social justice. Social injustices included the limitation of rights to millions of Ivoirians, denying them passports, national identification cards, and national services to prevent them from making claims to important common resources which they otherwise were entitled to as citizens.

Autocracy and Dictatorship

Before and during the presidential conflict, the behavior of Ivoirian political leaders showed that autocracy and dictatorship were alive and well. This is most probably because it is extremely difficult to wean powerful leaders from autocratic and dictatorial propensities. Autocratic and dictatorial processes were intricately woven into the Ivoirian psyche, as much as into other West African/African experiences. The propensity for this behavior guided Gbagbo's inflexibility. In a democratic scenario, mediation and negotiation are generally important ways to resolve issues, but when autocratic and dictatorial propensities exist, the desire to use violence to resolve conflict increases on both sides.

Moreover, when Gbagbo took office, there was nothing that would have suggested to Ivoirians that he would eventually exhibit autocratic and dictatorial propensities. This phenomenon emerged as he developed longevity in the presidency and convinced himself and others that no one else could run Côte d'Ivoire effectively but himself. Gbagbo displayed all the elements of autocratic and dictatorial power when he manipulated conditions. He refused to call for elections from 2005 until 2010 because he thought things may be advantageous to him. During the conflict, he nullified election results in several regions of the country and coerced the court to declare him the winner. Furthermore, he forced citizens to accept instability, empowered deadly militias (including the Young Patriots) onto Ivoirian streets, and sanctioned several massacres.

As Gbagbo became more desperate, he began to employ more coercive tactics to punish his opponents and to solidify his entrenchment in the presidency. From 2005 to 2010 he disregarded years of negotiated agreements to make substantive changes, and during the presidential conflict he also disregarded the AU, ECOWAS, and the UN, hoping the tactic would eventually work to his favor.

Autocracy and dictatorship manifest in several ways. Two may be applicable here. One way is the deliberate intention of dictator leaders (Fidel Castro, Gaddafi of Libya, Mubarak of Egypt, Omar al-Bashir of Sudan, Bashar al-Assad of Syria, the previous military junta in Myanmar, and so many others) to seize and stay in power indefinitely. The other way occurs when potential leaders masquerade as the people's democratic liberators (Fidel Castro and Gbagbo), while secretly craving indefinite control of power.

Undergirding the two forms are the assumption that citizens are ignorant and incapable of governing, protecting, and sustaining themselves.

In the beginning, many Ivoirians accepted that Gbagbo had democratic aspirations. He appeared with credentials that guaranteed some measure of trust from Ivoirians. He had been a professor of history, and had published several books mostly dealing with freedom, democracy, and good governance. He had argued vehemently for multi-party system, civil society, and an electoral government in order to wean Côte d'Ivoire from the dictatorial and neo-colonial decades of Houphouët-Boigny.

Unfortunately, Gbagbo embraced dictatorial appetite and consequently personalized the presidency. Personalizing the presidency meant that he had to fight for his own survival. The near-successful coup of 2002 and the civil strife that followed were indications that his legacy had turned different groups across the nation into dissatisfied and bitter enemies. Instead of devoting time to the affairs of the nation, he focused on fighting opponents and imprisoning those whom he perceived to be dangerous to his autocratic and dictatorial ambitions.

Gbagbo's desire to remain president indefinitely was due to a number of factors. He had high contempt for several segments of the Ivoirian population, believed that no one else was capable of governing the nation, and he was not willing let go of the high privilege, power, and advantages that the office of the Ivoirian presidency offered. Also, he was tightly guarding his liberator status. He was the only one who dared challenge the dictator Houphouët-Boigny, but he incorrectly assumed that being a liberator with impracticable theoretical notions of democracy entitled him to an indefinite sojourn in the presidency. His presidency not only diminished the prospects of democracy, but also introduced socio-economic and socio-political challenges that increased divisiveness in the Ivoirian society.

The Absence of Women

Women's voices were absent in the crucial discourse of presidential governance in Côte d'Ivoire. The idea of establishing democracy in the nation was to introduce and sustain a diversity that respected ethnicities, gender, and religion. Unfortunately, the successive masculine domination of the presidency, the specific entrance of Gbagbo onto the scene, and the presidential conflict removed all prospects of women's participation. Even after the presidential conflict was resolved with violence, Ouattara appointed a male to the prime minister position, showing that he was not interested in clean democracy or the kind of inclusivity that recognized women as equal players.

The exclusion of women from the highest office of political governance spans from the time of independence from France all through to Gbagbo and Ouattara. The blatant masculine domination only gave access to a few women in lower leadership positions. Among the 320 families that dominated the Ivoirian governance system since the time of Houphouët-Boigny (Tessilimi 1984, 24), women were never included in the two top positions (president and prime minister).

Transitional Disjunction

Finally, each time a new government came to power, the efforts and achievement of the old regime got thrown out. The new team makes no effort to sustain continuity. The ruling elite in Côte d'Ivoire demonstrated this phenomenon right from the beginning of the death of Houphouët-Boigny through Gbagbo's and Ouattara's presidency. Each incoming president harbored intense animosity against the other and disinterest in the previous regime's positive contribution, thereby unwittingly dislocating unity, coherence, and opportunities for national development.

Harms from the Negative Use of Power

The harms caused by the negative use of political power are often associated with the scourge of authoritarianism and inflexible political governance. Inclement conditions in fragile economies often bring about competition, especially as people struggle to survive by any means necessary. In those scenarios, the "survival of the fittest" takes precedence. The looting of the Ivoirian treasury by the political elite was a display of the negative use of political power. Conversely, the looting that occurred on the part of the poorer populations was associated with the competition for food and other material resources they never had. Conflict scenarios are usually fecund contexts for adverse economic, social, and political activities that cause more damage to already precarious conditions.

The negative use of power creates antagonistic rather than collaborative interaction. Many of those who had political power in Côte d'Ivoire took advantage of the adversarial scenario and looted government coffers for their personal benefit. Those who did not have mandated political power constructed power by drawing on negative ideologies to become agents of violence and death. Looting government coffers translated into less money for mending social inequalities and national development.

The specific behavior to loot or burn down buildings was understandably driven by anger that simmered within disadvantaged Ivoirians for a long time. Even though not everyone in the disadvantaged population acted in ways that defied civility, those who engaged in violence created added strain on the already tenuous socio-economic conditions. These conditions caused fear, displacement, and dispersal. Displacement and dispersal were the direct result of fear, so many Ivoirians packed up what few belongings they had and left the context of violence to become refugees in neighboring nations.

The presidential conflict empowered the "survival of the fittest" mentality allowing political and other elites to demand privileges and advantages. They formed rings of protection around themselves, and drew upon resources in ways that most citizens could not. Privileges and advantages included using the military and police to defend their premises and to go after those who opposed them or posed threats. Ivoirian political elites were also protected by friendly external nations, guaranteeing many of them access to safe havens when needed.

By 2010/2011 Côte d'Ivoire was considered a fragile nation. In fragile nations, violence is the preferred form of conflict resolution. Violence never resolves conflict. Certainly, Gbagbo and Ouattara had Gandhi's and King's nonviolence approaches. Yet during their conflict, Gbagbo and Ouattara, who are supposedly well-educated, and for years enjoyed the fruits of civil arrangements abroad (France and the United States), chose to use violence as their form of conflict resolution. They were so focused on their subjective positions that the negation of each other drove them in the end to impose might, power, and violence.

Negation is a form of social and political tactic that enforces polarization and increases alienation. Alienation had two purposes in this conflict. Even though it helped in isolating both presidents from each other, it also helped in increasing the popularity of their respective ideologies. The more an ideological position was acceptable to adherents, the more divisions occurred between conflict parties and their adherents.

Furthermore, in Côte d'Ivoire, alienation produced some adverse consequences, such as the neglect of citizens' basic needs, and the neglect of critical essential national affairs such as ensuring that labor, service, and the protection of production mechanisms remained consistent. Alienation polarized ethnic groups and forced Ivoirians to become suspicious and distrustful of each other. Such distrust and suspicions led to denial of access (to many northerners, some of whom were half Ivoirian), intimidation, and consequently violence.

The legal system was also manipulated, forcing it to deviate from its function as the applicator of impartial rules. Following the easy acquiescence of the judges to rule in Gbagbo's favor, the Ivoirian justice system appeared set up to sustain dictatorial governance. Thus, the presidential conflict increased inconsistent legal conditions, forcing the Ivoirian legal community to disregard useful impartiality to opt for partiality with negative ramifications.

As well, the promises (introduce democracy, economic advancement, infrastructural development, and justice for all) upon which individuals come to power were not adequately reviewed before people voted individuals into governance roles. Most citizens do not have statistical data or the statistical tools for such evaluations. It follows then that was never a defined, self-sustaining democratic character in Côte d'Ivoire because citizens relied on emotive promises. Moreover, the nation also relied on assistance from its colonial master, France, as well as assistance from international monetary systems and humanitarian groups. From 1993 after the death of its first president, every crisis became a step downward in terms of national advancement and support so that a once-thriving Côte d'Ivoire in the 1970s and early 1980s became (exacerbated by the presidential conflict) a fragile nation by 2010 and 2011.

It is useful to mention that for several African nations, the assistance from the World Bank and the IMF generally enriched political elites at the expense of ordinary citizens. The IMF, a traditional neo-imperial monetary powerhouse, makes its revenue by coercing weakened or fragile nations to accept high-interest loans with high loan repayment conditions. Also, the IMF forces these broken nations to accept structural adjustments (austerity measures) which consequently impoverish citizens.

For weakened and fragile nations, monetary loans and repayment conditions have traditionally detracted from internal economic productivity. Paying back loans and trying to look good before a powerful global monetary system, which often destroys nations' credibility if they default or slow down in the repayment process, often diminishes responsibility to internal national needs. In the end, these fragile nations experience various levels of social, political, and economic disruptions or collapse.

During the presidential conflict, the World Bank and the IMF were present in the nation, worried about previous loans, while across the nation, educational options such as school attendance were disrupted, and healthcare services diminished. As with any civil strife, safe traveling across the nation with public transportation became a challenge (some of the roads were bad and dangerous), with increased fear on the part of already vulnerable Ivoirians who had been targeted by Ivoirité for years. Because this was a masculine political regime at war, even the small efforts to equalize opportunities between women and men were disrupted and relegated to the background. However, despite the impact of adverse consequences wrought by the presidential conflict (high unemployment, infrastructural damage due to violence, increased poverty, insecurity, and instability), the structure of the Ivoirian economic system has potential to eventually sustain economic growth.

Chapter Nine

An Africa Conflict Transformation Model

This book examined the conflict between presidents Gbagbo and Ouattara of Côte d'Ivoire and found that the conflict tracks back to a series of issues embedded in Ivoirian national history. President Gbagbo's inflexible response to the election results in 2010 led to an intractable conflict that was shut down with violence. The UN Security Council (March 2011) gave a clear description of all the events that were enacted to try to resolve the conflict. Following the UN description, Gbagbo was clearly in the wrong. He lost the second round of the elections, and his opponent, Ouattara, was declared legitimate president-elect by the Ivoirian electoral commission, the UN on December 3, 2010, and the AU, EU, and the United States.

On December 7 2010, ECOWAS endorsed Ouattara as president-elect and called on Gbagbo to step down. On December 9, the AU agreed with ECOWAS, and called on Gbagbo to step down. On December 20 and 21, the EU and the United States imposed visa bans on Gbagbo, his wife, and several individuals. The United States imposed economic sanctions, and thirteen of the twenty private banks doing business in Côte d'Ivoire closed up shop (United Nations Security Council 2011b). This move was clearly a squeeze to get Gbagbo to step down. Such moves though, generally increase conflict intractability. International and diplomatic efforts worked tirelessly to get Gbagbo to understand the unfair nature of his claim to the presidency to no avail.

The AU and ECOWAS were in the forefront in trying to mitigate the conflict. Different popular leaders from Thabo Mbeki, former president of South Africa, and Olusegun Obasanjo, former president of Nigeria, added to the consistent AU and ECOWAS negotiations, meetings, and assessments of the situation on the ground. On March 24, 2011, the ECOWAS heads of states finally decided time was up and Gbagbo had to go. They followed their very strong resolution by requesting the UNOCI to empower UN peace keepers to protect civilians (United Nations Security Council 2011b). The AU and ECOWAS delegates proactively met approximately ten times as they tried to resolve the conflict. With the notion that these groups tried to resolve the presidential conflict with a European-style diplomatic approach, it was necessary to develop a conflict model that takes into consideration some African traditional elements. This model may be useful for mitigating similar conflicts in the future.

The Africa Village Conflict Transformation model (AVCT) is designed to only respond to conflict between two parties where one party is clearly making a wrong claim. The model is unique because it was developed in view of presidential conflict in Côte d'Ivoire. The AVCT has the following components. The first and most important element of the model is that village elders serve as mediators (AU and ECOWAS leaders) and observers must immediately respond by entering the conflict context to ensure that instability does not break out among conflict parties' supporters. In addition, contrary to the idea that Westerners and other expatriates are used to being immediately repatriated back to safety somewhere, the international community should send observer delegates from every part of the world to keep vigil, support systems, and encourage safety, rule of law, and continuity.

In the case of the Ivoirian presidential conflict, even though there were elders (AU and ECOWAS members) who worked tirelessly to try to get a resolution, they left out two important factors: a clear conflict map, and a less guilty/antagonistic approach. The conflict negotiation was taken over by aggressive international political leaders and diplomats. Many of these individuals harbored autocratic and dictatorial sentiments, and had the interests of powerful nations and corporations at heart.

When conflict parties are hurried into a quick resolution because international leaders, diplomats, and corporations that want business and natural resources to keep flowing uninterruptedly are involved, then it is most likely that such a conflict would become more intractable, the solution of which can only be violence. Violence, the final solution in Côte d'Ivoire, is never a proper way to resolve conflict. Improperly resolved conflict is a recipe for the discontent of both or one of the conflict parties, portending the eventual resurfacing of the conflict. Clearly, the post-conflict scenario in Côte d'Ivoire demonstrates this phenomenon (United Nations Security Council 2011a). This phenomenon is also evident in Sudan, Rwanda, Kosovo, Congo, and Bosnia, where populations remain antagonistic to each other, and are only kept from dismembering each other by AU, UN, and NATO peacekeeping forces who can only varnish over the animosity with temporary protection.

The first process in the AVCT model is that the village elders are truthfully briefed as to the complexity of the conflict (no propaganda or clandestine agenda, nor partiality to any of the conflict parties). Such intense truthful briefing should generally take a few days, but must only occur after clear information and understanding of the positions of both conflict parties. The next important step is the immediate isolation of both conflict parties to a remote neutral context. The elders (in this case, AU, ECOWAS members) determine instantly a trustworthy and seasoned interim neutral leadership team from within the nation, who temporarily keep things going while the conflict parties have been invited and moved to a neutral place for consistent conversations. This is extremely important because economic, political, and social continuity is crucial for moving the nation along during the conflict.

Once the conflict parties are removed from the conflict context, then the mediation work of getting to a resolution begins. It is important that they are in a completely neutral place and surrounded by neutral facilitators who only work on logistics and comfort issues. Since they are no longer in leadership positions, all their communication tools, cell phones, and so on are removed, not because they are being punished but because the priority is to get to a workable, reasonable transformation of the conflict which is more important than anything else.

During the presidential conflict, the AU, ECOWAS, and the UN, with all their might and global power, did not think to remove Gbagbo and Ouattara from the conflict context. Even though these elders agreed that Gbagbo was in the wrong, and that Ouattara was somewhat the legitimate president-elect, leaving the two presidents in the conflict context to keep communicating with their different armed supporters led to violence and other socio-economic and socio-political consequences. In addition to the violence, the presidents were themselves shortsighted, confused, and continually disrupted in terms of carrying out simple governance logistics. It was clearly difficult for Ouattara to run a country from a hotel, and for Gbagbo to run a country holed up in the presidential residence.

The point of this model is that their removal from the conflict context and their replacement with a neutral interim leadership team may have been advantageous to Côte d'Ivoire in terms of economic and social stability. And whatever the interim leadership team sets in motion would have been fluidly continued by the rightful president once the conflict was resolved.

The next useful dynamic of the AVCT model is the deliberation period, which allows the mediation elders to accurately judge the circumstances and make an immediate substantive decision as to who the culprit is in the conflict. This approach immediately separates this model from other conflict resolution models. This is a very specific kind of conflict, and following Iris Marion Young's *Responsibility for Justice* (2011), the conflict elders are not looking for a guilty culprit to punish. Instead, this is a scenario where the culprit is attached to a high level of responsibility to others (Ivoirians, Africa, and the globe), which empowers a recognition of the culpability and a need for an immediate transformation of behavior.

Now punishment is useless in the search for such a transformative restitution process. The idea is to engage the conflict party who is in the wrong with a series of discourses on accepting the responsibility for their position, and to convince them to see and understand that there is something fundamentally wrong with that conception of events. Once the party in the wrong comes to this understanding and agreement, then the outcome of the acceptance of culpability should not be punishment, but a chance to connect the individual back to the society. Young (2011) points to the dynamics of connective responsibility as something that energizes everyone and creates a new vista for collaborative problem transformation.

Another way to think about this aspect of the model is to consider the scenario in terms of two children in the same family fighting about something, and clearly one of them is in the wrong but insists that he or she is right. In families, the parents are the elders who always serve as mediators to help children see and understand problems properly. Like Gbagbo, most children are usually very stubborn, but just imagine that the culprit child accepts responsibility for being wrong. Would the next step be that the parents proceed to assault the child because the child admits guilt and must be punished following popular retributive-justice models? Or should the next step be that the parents admonish both children to learn to treat each other with dignity, respect, and a level of connective responsibility?

The third step of the model is that as soon as acceptance of culpability occurs, instead of thinking punishment, festivities and celebration of the courage of the culprit to come to that recognition and conclusion takes precedence. The recognition of culpability is the beginning of the end of the conflict. Immediate national and international announcements are made that the conflict party determined to be in the wrong all along has in a neutral mediational context accepted culpability, and that the nation can rejoice and begin to steady itself in terms of moving forward with national development and its democratic aspirations. That is also an indication that the culprit party is to be fully welcomed back into the national fold.

This model draws from the South African model of conflict transformation. In South Africa, toward the end of the apartheid system, instead of indigenous Africans launching brutal attacks on whites who had tortured them for about 350 years (see Terreblanche 2002), they were encouraged to use their *Ubuntu* philosophy (Tutu 1999) to embrace everyone. This was a very difficult, painful, but conscious and compassionate conflict resolution approach. Instead of punishment or retribution, white South Africans were given connective love (forgiveness and reconciliation) that encouraged them internally, from 1994 (when Mandela became president) to the present, to continually struggle to relinquish the shortcomings of the past in view of a collaborative present and a productive future.

The last part of the model is that both conflict parties would come together to work out the details of what they can give and take from each other in terms of diminishing or even eliminating animosity. Keep in mind that even the person in the wrong has followers and that these followers are equally citizens; though perceptually viewed by the other party to be misguided, they must be treated with dignity and responsibly incorporated into the national experience.

The AVCT model is different from the popular models of mediation because it quickly gathers evidence to determine who is in the wrong. From that point on, the elders proceed to actively interact with both conflict parties in dynamic, creative, and traditionally African ways (emphasizing their connection to each other, compassion, and care—*Ubuntu*) until the best possible scenario for national stability is agreed upon by the conflict parties.

Western models approach conflicts by first mapping them, and then finding a conflict resolution approach that would best respond to the conflict. In this way options for conflict resolution after mapping include mediation, negotiation, and facilitation. In contrast, the AVCT model has three distinct periods, and a simple rather than a complicated matrix is preferred. The three periods are clear: (1) the starting point is where all parties involved in the conflict are given notice of what is about to occur, (2) the second period is where trusted village members determine where the problem lies, and (3) the third period is where the actual linking together of everyone in the conflict occurs in view of the conflict resolution and a positive face-saving conclusion. The first two periods serve as the mapping of the conflict, and the last period is the actual work of getting to an outcome.

Because the model is responding to a very particular kind of conflict, a conflict where one individual is clearly in the wrong, it combines practices from popular mediation, negotiation, and facilitation approaches. In this model, the conflict parties do not have to be at the table or floor at all times. The model is actuated by extremely trusted "village members" or elders (in this case, AU, ECOWAS, and anyone else they want to invite from the UN) who in turn move back and forth between the two parties, but focus more time on the party that is clearly in the wrong. The mapping begins by determining which party is in the wrong, and all-out efforts are placed on getting that party to understand that its position is problematic and wrong.

Like the principled and integrative negotiation approach, the AVCT model is also seeking a "win-win" scenario, albeit from a different perspective. The model focuses on teasing out an outcome that has substantive benefits to all parties. In the third segment, the "village" (mediation and negotiating teams) ensures that both parties come away with beneficial conditions in ways that no one can claim absolute victory. Even though Ivoirians and the international community were perturbed by the presidential conflict, the AVCT model views the conflict as a complete misunderstanding based on inherited, fragmented governance and political ideologies. The internalization of these ideologies created the stifling disjuncture that resulted in the standoff between Gbagbo and Ouattara. The AVCT model would ensure that the conflict outcome gives all parties some level of victory because they all should have worked on various aspects of the conflict transformation, including their behaviors and the terms of the final agreement.

The idea of the village is based on the notion of integration. In the village, almost everyone knows everyone, and people generally work somewhat well together. The AU and ECOWAS were quick to forget that they had powerful African models of conflict transformations such as *Ubuntu*. Instead, they impatiently involved the UN and other international groups, which generally default to conflict resolution with threats, deadlines, and violence.

RATIONALE OF THE AVCT MODEL

The AVCT model is a form of liberation mediation. Accepting culpability is the beginning part of liberation, sort of the beginning of new knowledge and awareness. Rejecting that one is wrong or accepting culpability occurs through a series of steps which begin by first recognizing the subjective conclusions that undergird one's position. The other steps involve understanding why it is important that such a conviction no longer has a place in the village, the nation, and the world at large. Upon recognizing the wrong, the party in the wrong must then proceed to carefully articulate why it is now rejecting that position. It must also clearly say what such understanding does subjectively and collectively to the individual and the entire nation. Were Gbagbo to be evaluated with AVCT, he would have had to come to a conclusion that there is a fundamental difference between forcing oneself on a nation as the powerful and almighty ruler, and the humility that guides a true leader to recognize that something is not quite right when a sizeable number of citizens no longer want someone as a leader.

The AVCT model also seeks to ensure that the conflict party in the wrong distinguishes between personal and subjective privileges which may be pursued through other means rather than using the people's collective governance. Additional steps in the model are that once the party in the wrong accepts culpability, then apologies follow. First apology goes to the other conflict party, then to the village elders, then to the nation, and then to the international community. This is to inform them of what went wrong and why it is now important to sustain collective progress and to respect civil society, fairness, and specifically the rule of fair laws governing national and international coherence.

The AVCT model is aware that this elaborate apology process is an expiation and a commitment to the service of social, economic, and political coherence. The outcome of the interaction gives both parties a chance to renew faith in each other as people who, given the proper conditions, really care for each other and for their nation. After the apology process, a national holiday is declared, and the nation engages in massive celebrations. A special medal of courage, honor, humility, and service to the nation is given to the party who was once in the wrong. As a form of respect for what they achieved, they are given special lifetime privileges. This kind of recognition is important because it emphasizes that individuals who have served their nations, corporations, or systems can make mistakes. But what is important is the courage to recognize their wrong. Such individuals become model citizens capable of change, capable of telling the truth, capable of seeing wrong from right, and capable of reconciliation. They also become a beacon of light for all the young people who are always seeking directions to walk fairly in their advancement to adulthood.

The AVCT model shifts people from corruptive discourse and dictatorial psychology to collaborative humility. Young people begin to learn that accepting to be wrong and accounting for it is actually useful and life-enhancing. As in a typical "real" family context, when individuals are clearly seen to be wrong and are given the chance to state their conviction, and then carefully and meticulously, they are shown how they are in the wrong. In this way people tend to do better. The other important part of the village conflict model is that the wise elders of women and men are very aware that a minority or an individual may be in the right, and that the entire nation may be in the wrong. If the conflict is between a large system and an individual, especially when power dynamics are involved, the village may still try to find the key people in the large and powerful system and approach them the same way it would approach any party. The same conditions will hold, and the idea is to try to convince the large and powerful system that it is on the wrong side and get it to relinquish that behavior.

In the case of Côte d'Ivoire, many young people (Young Patriots and others) have already been socialized into a dangerous fragmented experience that may be hard to shake. When such individuals become political leaders, they may only have aggression and anger from which to draw their responses. Western education and practices have proven to be important but were not quite helpful in terms of the progressive decisions that led to the conflict between Gbagbo and Ouattara who were quintessential, hyper-Western-educated Ivoirians. Somehow, additional ways of dealing with political conflict, creating pools of knowledge of best practices, and creating ways to extract significant lessons from history are going to be very important as options for young Ivoirians. From these pools of resources, they can draw important lessons to enact transformative socio-economic and socio-political dynamic processes that focus specifically on national development. The AVCT model is a prolegomenon to several other models that may appear in the future.

Interactive Prescriptions

Before discussing prescriptions, a few general comments regarding governance, citizenship, and responsibility with regard to Côte d'Ivoire are in order. It appears that in Côte d'Ivoire, because of the colonial, post-colonial, and the intermixing of contemporary and colonial heritages, citizens are socialized to expect government and political leaders to carry out all the responsibilities of social development and national progress. This is also a West Africa/African phenomenon. In other words, without the government and political leaders, important things never get done. This is a critical problem that leaches into the nature of individual and collective self-determination. It follows that individuals never quite view themselves as empowered enough to drive some amount of self- and local development. For instance, when the fragile infrastructure breaks down, citizens mostly sit around waiting and assuming that the government is the only source of solutions. This unidirectional dichotomy between citizens and the government creates additional conditions that immobilize citizens during civil conflict, forcing most of them to be personally unresponsive and dependent.

All across Côte d'Ivoire and other West African/African nations, mostly poor individuals set up very small-scale subjective street trading activities such as selling fruits, vegetables, cigarettes, candy, and music/music accessories. This is an indication that many poor Ivoirians (and other Africans) have not been encouraged with the tools of constructive education/skills to pursue self-mobilized large-scale activities that are beneficial to individuals and communities.

The presence of self-determining and self-sustaining educational and economic activities generally sustains communities when governments are in transition or collapse. Here the notion of Sen's (1999, 2001) freedom and individual capabilities is useful. Individual capabilities, linked to collective community capabilities, would help shift Ivoirians and many other Africans from the mentality of idling around always waiting or relying on government for solutions. All kinds of transformation required in Côte d'Ivoire, and other African nations for that matter, go way beyond what a few political elites are willing to provide or can provide. Self-determining individual and self-determining collective educational, economic, and other actions may be the catalyst that would breed the kind of development that is less dependent on elite governance, but is at once somewhat sustaining, liberating, and transforming.

In other words, dependency on the government increases when there is minimal personal responsibility on the part of citizens, and it is worse when resources are also constantly donated from external sources. As long as citizens internalize the idea that government and political elites are the only ones who can supply answers to desired changes in terms of creating opportunities for sustainable education, jobs, social security, quality of life, and self-determination, then very little actual transformation may be expected. The other side of this coerced dependency problem is that it empowers the political elite to entrench itself through increased false and empty promises. Believing that citizens are always relying on the crumbs it provides, political leaders get caught up in increased tragic shortsightedness that neglects the power of the people in co-governance and co-development of the nation. Unwittingly these political leaders increase their belief that the government through them is always the arbitrary benefactor to masses of incapacitated citizens.

Closely linked to mobilizing citizens to enlarge national development enterprises is the question of mobilizing for crisis responsibilities. Generally, citizens who wait for internal and external remedies are also impoverished in terms of how to deal with internal conflict. From about December of 2010 through March of 2011, both presidents maintained stifling inflexibility against each other, refusing to enter into negotiations to end the conflict. Because their internalized perceptions of power did not allow a fruitful negotiation, the conflict was only resolved with violence.

Moreover, it is important to clarify that social justice is not simply the provision of government food stamps or the default to government responsibility for the totality of economic, political, and social life. Social justice is a voluntary and fundamental activity brought about not by humanitarian groups constantly traversing fragile nations alone, or by government or foreign government aid, but by the actions of citizens focused on getting everyone to respect the fair distribution of the common resources of their specific contexts. Self-determining social justice actions construct buffer zones that protect citizens in times of prosperity or of need. But when a government such as that of Côte d'Ivoire coerces citizens to depend on it, but provides little or no stability in terms of encouraging distributive justice (social justice), then the citizens' capabilities for constructing self-determining social justice is questionable. Naturally, a government that hears that it needs to encourage social justice gets defensive. This is because most political leaders misunderstand social justice and construe it as a government and/or humanitarian activity to sustain just the poor. That misunderstanding has been devastating to fragile nations. All good governments need to do is to encourage and ensure that citizens are fair to each other. In addition, good governments, appropriately using taxpayers' revenue, ought to provide supporting economic grants that help and increase communities' self-sustaining social justice efforts. Good governments are also conscious that the self-determining social justice efforts are protective of all citizens' dignity and rights. Good governments are always open to challenges that seek to correct government political improprieties that may be harmful to citizens' freedoms and self-determination.

When social justice is not taken seriously, it simply means that human rights and dignity violations, as well as other forms of harm are allowed to flourish. In Côte d'Ivoire, the government appeared oblivious to the importance of social justice. This underscores that point regarding citizens' capabilities. Were Ivoirians to have robust self-determining programs, the responsibility of support and sustenance may not have been that desperate. Instead, it took the support of social justice–based humanitarian organizations to temporarily create inclusive access to basic common resources such as water, food, and healthcare.

However, new forms of transformative discourses may need to be as basic as aggressive community literacy programs such as those enacted by Paulo Freire as explained in his *Pedagogy of the Oppressed* (1990). It may also be enhanced by Burggraeve's *From Self Responsibility to Solidarity* (1985). Freire and Burggraeve both insist that one's relationship with other human beings is always important in the transformative process. While empowerment and transformation is occurring, scholars and practitioners working in fragile nations would also need to move away from the discourse of blame (of the government, of colonial and neo-colonial systems, of the elite, of corrupt groups, and so on) and focus on liberatory discussions and models that would help draw out the creative and collaborative power within citizens while also simultaneously connecting them together. This type of connective responsibility has also been expressed by Iris Marion Young (2011).

So what kind of prescriptions would be useful for Côte d'Ivoire following the findings from the presidential conflict? The United Nations, for instance, already has the UNOCI, which is supposed to target precise responsibilities ranging from socio-political stability to ensuring the enactment and continuity of democratic ideals and civil society in Côte d'Ivoire. Additional prescriptions may require specific safeguards, measured and monitored with best-practice rubrics by a collaboration of seasoned internal and external nongovernmental support systems. This approach is only temporary and ought to empower internal agents to take over their own self-determination and monitoring. This safeguard would continually monitor governance behavior and ensure positive outcomes at all times.

Côte d'Ivoire may seek a different approach to prescriptions. For instance, it could abandon Western interaction altogether and move to test new ideas. It could insist that its problems have arisen because the nation abandoned its African traditional roots and ways to adopt Western (French) approaches and procedures, which appear to have adversely affected them. For this reason, a shift to an Afrocentric socio-economic and socio-political system may be helpful. Côte d'Ivoire has plenty of resources from which to draw practices and procedures. *Ubuntu* of South Africa is especially a powerful guide. Falling back to roots and the Bob Marley idea of "Africa unite" does not mean that Africans are to estrange themselves from external interactions; it just means that they need their own substantive Afrocentric foundation from which to operate their economic, political, and social systems.

The idea of this prescription is to get Ivoirians doing the same things that other groups already do well. Russia, China, and India are classic examples of nations using a deep sense of their specific socio-cultural identities formalized by language, writing, traditions, and copious historical support. Afrocentric self-determination for Ivoirians would be partly a way to get out of the quagmire of having to depend on Western systems that are mostly incompatible with the Ivoirian context. This also means that they would have to wean themselves from social and political apathy that has entangled them against each other, often involving the Western world as referees or liberators. More importantly, this suggestive prescription may be a pathway to recapturing the significance of personal links to each other. In other words, Ivoirians need to develop an indigenous response to their internal challenges.

Of course, the idea of Ivoirians generating an Afrocentric governance system may receive adverse reactions internally and externally. The idea may be contested because Africa continues to be perceived by the global community as a continent that cannot rise out of the ashes of colonial, post-colonial, corruptive, and dictatorial malevolence. That idea is sustained by the presence of Westerners in Africa observing and documenting for Africans (no matter how problematic their views are) human-rights abuses and making video documentaries about conditions (for instance wars) that have raged on for decades (see Russell 2012a, 2012b). Therefore, the call for Afrocentric or indigenous self-determination as prescription to strengthen Côte d'Ivoire would be seen as a wrongheaded proposal because Africans cannot ever sever themselves from the Western world or the global community for that matter.

To scare Ivoirians away from adopting an Afrocentric prescription, people may be asked to imagine a nation where ethnocentric and religious wars explode, causing a hastily dying Côte d'Ivoire to be consumed with chaos. In such a scenario, the already challenged governance system becomes more corruptive and normalizes violence, massive death, and huge migration to neighboring nations which would create massive humanitarian crises. And since Western nations do not want to be inundated with the immigration strain of fragile/poor Africans mostly considered to be "global liabilities," they would be the first to discourage such a move as suicidal.

A reasonable, workable, but challenging prescriptive option would be the blending of perspectives. This would mean carefully drawing from the very best of Afrocentric dynamics (traditional compassion, care for the village, "it takes a village," and traditional sharing of resources), and constructing a syncretistic response by linking them to the best practices of other global options found to be culturally, economically, and politically useful. For instance, from the Western worldview, it can draw upon practices of strengthening production, labor, service, and efficient response relationships and combine those with African compassion, creativity, resilience, and ingenuity.

It is useful to suggest that most prescriptions, especially those offered in view of fragile nations, do face competition from external systems, specifically options offered by the IMF and the World Bank. These powerful institutions mostly focus on quick-fix measures that are advantageous to them and to Ivoirian political elites, but devastating to the larger Ivoirian population.

From a different angle, prescriptive options may be useful when there is a national character that curbs the inflexible desire to hold on to political power indefinitely and by all means. This important psychological phenomenon was captured early by the founding members who organized the U.S. Constitution. They understood at the time (1787) that for reasons linked to human nature (see Hume 1934), when individuals gain access to power and the privileges therein, it is often difficult to get them to step down without violence. The formation of the Constitution of the United States gave special space for the office of the presidency and insisted that it is to be occupied by one individual for four years, and at the end of that term, that individual may seek another and the last four-year term (U.S. Constitution, Article II Section 1, 1787; and the 20th Amendment 1933). This fundamental law has kept dangerous power-hungry psychopaths with raging dictatorial propensities to stay in office indefinitely away from the U.S. presidency.

Whereas in Côte d'Ivoire individuals who have been presidents several times continue to seek reelection, the Constitution of the United States does not provide any legal space or make amendment provision for an individual who has served as president in the past to try and come back to office. This is an excellent best practice that Ivoirians may want to carefully consider without imitating overt racial, gender, and monetary propensities that infiltrate the U.S. political scenario.

In the dynamics of national governance, especially with respect to the service of the presidency, individuals who are addicted to socio-political control and who seek to sit in power indefinitely (for instance, Gbagbo, Gaddafi, Syria's al-Assad, Sudan's Omar al-Bashir, and so on) completely miss the point about the nature of and the reason for the existence of a national government. While some nations insist on power nepotism, others, those not part of the eternal ruling elite and who manage to get into power, find ways to manipulate the system so that they stay in power indefinitely. When a dictator is challenged by any segment of society, instead of entering into interactive negotiation with citizens, the brutal assertion of power is preferred as an arbitrary quick fix. Such an approach to governance and its relationship with those governed misses the point of the nature of and use of government.

Since the Constitution of the United States has been drawn upon here as an example of a best practice in terms of presidential term limits, it is important to consider what the scenario would have been like today if the United States did not have individuals in the 1780s who creatively thought far ahead. It is possible that devastation and instability would have occurred because of extreme and unbridled racial, gender, ethnic, religious, and class animosities and insecurities. In addition, anger, antagonism, and violence may have been a staple diet were the U.S. system to be under successive dictatorship with individuals staying in the office of the presidency interminably.

Thus, even though prescriptive recommendations are fascinating, especially coming from outsiders, this book understands completely that the key to socio-political transformation lies in the minds and hands of Ivoirians. Only Ivoirians can organize themselves and strengthen their sensibilities in favor of respecting their own defined term limits, their rules of law, and the distributive justice that undergirds their national security. Instead of prescribing to Ivoirians what to do, perhaps a theoretical discussion of the consequences of dictatorial behavior in contemporary global arrangements may serve as useful historical lessons.

Lessons from History

Lessons from history are useful directions for individual and national progress. In Côte d'Ivoire, as in other African nations, respecting these lessons has been very challenging. Gbagbo was dissatisfied with the way things turned out. Instead of considering conciliatory and participatory democracy, he chose to deride Ivoirian citizens. He did not accept that most citizens knew what was good for them in terms of their choice of Ouattara as president. Unfortunately, Gbagbo allowed himself to be caught up in vapid insatiability, and tried to redefine political arrangements and behavior in his favor. His contentious behavior negated the very democracy and civility about which he wrote so well.

From the onset, it appeared that Gbagbo was not adequately and decisively informed by all groups attempting to negotiate with him that his conception of governance and use of political power was a problem. Instead, several groups, including the UN and AU, viewed him as an antagonistic individual. He was given several ultimatums by the international community. These ultimatums, as well as attempting to negotiate with Gbagbo in the context of UN, AU, and Western threats drove him into reclusion and intractability. There were never clear, responsible, and amicable statements and options internally or from the international community that may have lured Gbagbo to some level of reasonability.

In other words, even though Gbagbo was a political and economic liability, the groups which attempted to negotiate with him were also bellicose and inflexible. In conflict scenarios, response to aggression with aggression often begets more aggression. Consequently, the ACTM, as well as the interactive prescriptive options suggested in this book, are more in the direction of encouraging simple practical ways to philosophically think about the nature and implications of elite conflict. Prescriptive discussions are mostly about cautioning so that post-conflict lessons are easily appropriated in view of national progress, security, and justice for everyone. The overarching concern would always be what can be collaboratively and interactively done to respond to crisis while it is occurring, as well as after it has occurred.

However, because civil crises do occur and can turn fragile nations upside down, it may be useful to have crisis transformation systems in place. This is not a universal system, but one that takes the nuances of differing contexts into consideration, and is also flexible and responsive to the texture and ever-changing nature of conflict. This means that whenever conflict occurs (no matter how little or large), there ought to be diverse teams of crisis transformation experts whose sole mandate is transformation. Because Côte d'Ivoire did not have a system of crisis transformation beyond power-hungry and polarized police and military systems, when the presidential crisis arrived, various crucial systems shut down. The only help attempting to resolve the presidential conflict were aggressive international groups (the AU, ECOWAS, the EU, the United States, and the UN) and several humanitarian organizations.

In much of West Africa, individuals go after political power because of prestige and subjective privileges. Unfortunately, many of these individuals do not belong in government. Those who are in government are mostly not ready for the responsibilities and demands of good governance and civil society. Good governance requires special skills, commitment, and sacrifice all dedicated to serving citizens, immigrants, refugees, or visiting guests. Without the tactical and skillful ability to sustain a nation by implementing important stand-alone systems that can manage the nation in times of crisis, then disruption, chaos, and violence generally overwhelm everything.

The discourse about civil society is another way of pointing to leadership qualities. In addition to other connective responsible actions, good governance is really about setting up stand-alone structures and mechanisms so that when crisis occurs, the nation continues to function, and its schools, hospitals, airports, commerce, and especially assurance of social justice across the board provide uninterrupted services. This is the ideal and practicable image of good governance systems which ensure that systems exist to sustain citizens at all times, and can run consistently and independently of crisis conditions. Côte d'Ivoire certainly has the revenue (largest cocoa producer in the world) to enact substantive systems sufficiently sustained by self-sufficient government and positive private enterprises.

From a different angle, interactive prescriptive lessons may be drawn from other African contexts. Robert Mugabe fought for justice and yanked Rhodesia, later renamed Zimbabwe, from colonizers. After liberation, civil society and democracy reigned, but in time, President Mugabe morphed into a dictator. His creative vision of nationhood became a micro-vision of indefinite sojourn filled with an oppressive presidency. There are reasons why dictators stay on indefinitely. They do not want to relinquish power (Godwin 2011). They stay in power by insisting that they liberated the nation or some aspect of it from tyrants and oppressors. For Mugabe, this is true. So liberation groups such as Namibia's SWAPO, Mozambique's FRELIMO, Angola's UNITA, Zimbabwe's ZANU-PF, and South Africa's ANC are all still in power based on the liberator ideology So, the leaders of these organizations stay in power indefinitely or insist that their political groups continue to be in power (Godwin 2011).

However, Mugabe's myopic and uncompromising political governance behavior led to a collapse of the glorious nation he created. Even though President Mugabe is still in power, most of the critical labor force has left the country and migrated to seek economic opportunities in South Africa, Europe, North America, and Asia. The international community, especially the members with global economic and political clout, has simply shunned him, leaving him to preside over a fragile and ghost nation (see Godwin 2011).

It follows then that for liberation groups and leaders, any other group trying to get into political power may not understand the importance of liberation and so may lead the nation back into the hands of external oppressors. Clearly, Gbagbo viewed his political journey as an important liberatory effort that liberated the nation from a dictator (Houphouët-Boigny) who was closely linked to colonial and post-colonial grids. Unfortunately, once in power he believed that he was the only one who could legitimately govern the nation, and so prevented others from hijacking the nation and returning it back to dictatorial conditions. To achieve this, Gbagbo had to be a dictator. His move was probably the worst way to sustain his notion of democracy.

The South Africa story is a specifically useful lesson as a reminder that apartheid was utterly brutal, but collapsed despite all efforts by the Afrikaners and their internal and external supporters to sustain it. The leaders of the apartheid system were despicable dictators who eventually became an international embarrassment. But the uniqueness of the South Africa conflict was in the willingness of some of its key leaders to enter into negotiation when they saw the writing on the wall. The conclusion of that conflict and the outcome that has become the new South Africa is an excellent lesson in how people who once enjoyed unprecedented power must quickly learn to submit to reason and collaborate to cause collective transformation (see Terreblanche 2002).

In Egypt, the dictator Mubarak was chased out of office by dissatisfied and fed-up citizens. Both Tunisia and Egypt repeatedly mention their yearning and desire for social justice. As for Libya, Gaddafi was so sure that his dictatorial power was enough to intimidate the Libyan people that he refused to step down even in the face of a massive national revolution against him. Gaddafi had badly miscalculated the anger of the people and shortly after his capture was violently murdered because he was too arrogant to understand that dictators are unwelcome in contemporary global arrangements. Gbagbo was extremely lucky that he was captured alive and kept alive under the strict injunction of President Ouattara, who later handed him over to the International Criminal Court in The Hague to be tried for crimes against humanity.

In the Nigeria scenario, successive military dictators and coups destabilized the nation for more than three decades. It was not until its citizens decided to abandon military dictatorship and opted for a civilian governance system with presidential term limits that things began to calm down. But even with a thriving civilian governance system in place, the amount of chaos and conflict between groups still poses tremendous challenges for anyone working to get civil society, transformative resolution, and the respect of self-determination in place. It is ironic that while Nigeria is trying to create a civil society with democratic ideals, the Boko Haram (this name means Western education is sacrilegious), an Islamic extremist group, is trying to violently force the nation (bombing of government building, schools, market places, expatriate, and Christian religious institutions) to become an Islamic nation under sharia law and an Islamic religious dictatorship.

Liberia and Sierra Leone, Côte d'Ivoire's neighbors, went through massive civil strife and instability because the leaders sought total control, and taught that the use of brutal violence would lead to some sort of useful outcome to them. The only clearly visible outcome for both nations is the extreme poverty, the massive absence of infrastructure, and the national setback that has made both nations fragile countries. Wherever there are vestiges of dictatorships, including Syria and Russia, people have registered their concern and have posted notices through subtle or overt demonstrations that they no longer want such governance approaches.

To sum up this section, it may be useful to point out that the desire by some political elites to stay in presidential and other governance power indefinitely is sustained by their rejection of the lessons of history and by a feeling of invincibility over everyone else. These political elites often wrongly assume that the population needs elite leaders (no matter how bad or corrupt) to lead them. They also wrongly assume that keeping most citizens in massive poverty, undereducation, and ignorance is a sufficient buffer for guaranteeing allegiance and subordination. In addition, dictator liberators believe they are the only ones fit to lead, an illusion that fails to accept that many other citizens are equally capable of leadership roles. That illusion becomes a masculine manic rage whenever women enter the equation. Benazir Bhutto of Pakistan was murdered under such despondent masculine emotivism. In Côte d'Ivoire, women have been tactically precluded by elite male politicians from coming anywhere close to presidential governance. This is something, especially in terms of transformative justice, that Ouattara would need to consider if he is to be a true reformer.

From yet another angle, the lessons of history are neglected because many African dictators are empowered by the support of powerful advanced nations. This empowerment allows dictators to act with impunity, often violating the rights and dignity of their fellow citizens. Ironically, during peacetime, advanced nations draw tremendous benefits from cheap raw materials, cocoa and coffee in the case of Côte d'Ivoire, but during crises, the same nations sustain their revenue by supplying weapons to both sides of the conflict.

Most Ivoirians did not even understand that Gbagbo was consolidating himself as a dictator. His behavior appeared to be business as usual, and if he had been able to use his brutal power to eliminate Ouattara and other opposition, he may have continued as an autocratic and dictator president. Also, because Ouattara greatly desired the office of the presidency and was the legitimate president-elect, his move to consolidate a military front consisting of northern forces to oust Gbagbo, who had his own forces, risked a new civil war. Ouattara as much as Gbagbo believed in the use of violence as a form of conflict resolution. Ouattara's gamble only worked out because he was sustained by the UN, French troops, and other Western powers. Gbagbo was captured and eventually handed over to the ICC in The Hague. The question, of course, arises as to why Ivoirians cannot try Gbagbo in their own national court system. Instead they relinquish him to the ICC and play right into Gbagbo's views that former colonial powers still control African and African affairs.

However, the conflict between the two presidents had some serious damaging effects. Predictions about Ouattara's democratic or dictatorial behavior would need to wait until the end of his terms in office. Although it is doubtful that what occurred between Gbagbo and Ouattara would occur between Ouattara and some future presidential contender, autocracy and dictatorship are addictive diets and always nearby. Ouattara's success may be in his awareness that his behavior, policies, and actions ought to be aligned to sustain the lower stratum, developing a new generation of Ivoirian leaders (women and men), promoting civil society, and preparing to leave office at the end of his term.

The presidential conflict in Côte d'Ivoire was inevitable because there were circumstances before the conflict that already predetermined anyone who entered power to become addicted to dictatorial power. The conflict was also inevitable because as soon as Gbagbo entered power he did not fully understand that his theories and discourses on democracy needed to be concretized once he became president. If Gbagbo really understood participatory democracy, then he would have understood the rules and quickly stepped out of power when he lost in the second round of elections. Since he did not understand his own philosophy of democracy, it was not surprising that he easily defaulted to the dictatorial option and the use of violence.

As for Ouattara, he had become a hero among northern and other vilified Ivoirians, as well as neighboring nations (notably Burkina Faso). Such heroism requires him to show that he was the tough "big man" by acting decisively to resolve the presidential conflict. It is possible that an important motivator for ending the conflict with military violence rests on his business and economic perspectives. It is possible that Ouattara probably wanted to end the conflict as quickly as it started so as to reconnect his country back to the economic world.

Moreover, the presidential conflict is a reminder that autocratic dictatorship is an African problem with Mobutu Sese Seko of Congo, Idi Amin Dada of Uganda, Sani Abacha of Nigeria, and Robert Mugabe of Zimbabwe demonstrating the worst of this propensity. So far, the few nations (South Africa, Nigeria, Ghana, and a few others) sustaining the democratic process continue to be beacons of examples of emerging civil societies. The specific examples of Nelson Mandela, who relinquished power after four years of service, and Thabo Mbeki, who was relieved of service in his second term because of ethical impropriety, remain a good direction of how democracy should work in a civil society.

Finally, both presidents were at fault in different measures. Gbagbo made no effort to link his academic democratic discourse to Ivoirian reality; instead he entrenched a form of dictatorship. Ouattara was not patient enough to use exhaustive conflict transformation practice to try to lure Gbagbo into conciliatory negotiations; instead he too resorted to violence, which killed and displaced thousands of Ivoirians.

Most of those who tried to help with the conflict (UN, AU, EU, France, etc.) in terms of negotiations used gunboat diplomacy, a system that encourages haste, anger, and threats, which Gbagbo did not like and which pushed him to more intractability and violence. In the light of Mbeki's (2011) charge that there were too many unanswered questions, the complexity and implications of the conflict are going to be far reaching and much beyond the scope of this book. However, Mbeki's position does not nullify the fact that such conflicts may continue to occur because many African leaders are still wedded to very old and inflexible models of governance that insist on their negative use of political power.

Many autocratic and dictatorial African leaders supported by powerful external players are yet to understand and accept that shared governance and responsibility to the requirements of civil society are crucial for national development. They also fail to comprehend that the removal of subjective and personal pursuits while in political office helps to improve participatory self-determination, social justice options, and other useful conditions. This is what is expected from Ouattara, the current president of Côte d'Ivoire, and his governing team. Even though Mbeki (2011) suggested that Ouattara had been thrust into the Ivoirian presidency by the UN and other international stakeholders, Ouattara's behavior in office appears to be open to the notions of good governance, civil society, and some measure of inclusivity.

Conclusion

This book focused on the presidential conflict that occurred in Côte d'Ivoire between 2010 and 2011. Generally, internal national conflicts with international implications are of tremendous interest to governments across the world because useful lessons may be drawn and used to improve national social, economic, security, justice, and other concerns. The study was specifically interested in understanding the extent of the presidential conflict's impact on governance, political power, and social justice within the Ivoirian context. The study drew from numerous resources and concludes that the Gbagbo and Ouattara presidential conflict adversely affected or increased Ivoirian problems in terms of governance, political power, and social justice.

Even though the entire book is a historical critical discourse on the Ivoirian presidential conflict, several theories and a conflict-mapping model were added as evaluative tools. The discussion of the conflict led to the development of a new theory—"vapid insatiability theory"—and a new conflict model—the African conflict transformation model (ACTM). At the end of the book, interactive prescriptions were offered not as algorithmic solutions but as suggestive elements to consider before or during future similar conflict interaction.

However, the one important element to consider for Côte d'Ivoire, and for many other African nations, is the insistence on sustaining civil society, as well as democratic and universalizable rules that support all citizens across the board. Any package of good governance is always inclusive of peaceful transition and positive political responsibility. Several African nations have begun to embrace the value and content of peaceful transition and good governance. Since Jerry Rawlings's twenty-year autocratic rule in Ghana, that nation has settled on democratic succession. Nigeria's former president Goodluck Jonathan peacefully yielded power to President Muhammadu Buhari. South Africa, though racked with internal struggles, continues to insist on a peaceful transition of government which began with President Nelson Mandela to President Thabo Mbeki, and to President Jacob Zuma. The 2010–2011 Ivoirian presidential conflict is certainly filled with useful elements from which African leaders may draw lessons and chart more nuanced courses to comport themselves appropriately for the sake of their citizens rather than for subjective interests. This includes using national revenues and resources appropriately, and relinquishing power following the rules of democratic behavior.

Ultimately, positive fundamental civil society and democratic behavior would have tremendous benefits for individual African nations and their citizens seeking to expand, develop, and grow socially and economically. For Côte d'Ivoire, the eighteen-year sentence of General Bruno Dogbo Ble—head of Gbagbo's security detail (Ivory Coast Conflict 2017), the trials of former president Gbagbo and Blé Goudé at the International Court (ICC) in The Hague (Ba 2016), and the trial of Gbagbo's wife, Simone Gbagbo, in Côte d'Ivoire for crimes against the state and humanity (Ivory Coast's Former First Lady 2015) are useful indications of response to justice at large and social justice in particular.

Despite various crises since 2011, and most recently mutinous activities by some members of the military (Salau 2017), President Ouattara appears determined to help define current and future peaceful and democratic behavior and transition. Whichever direction Ouattara's presidency follows, his fascinating legacy of having endured the barbarization of his Ivoirian nationality (similar to President Obama of the United States) and religion may well be the crucible in which he institutionalizes better days and transformation for Côte d'Ivoire.

Similarly, his enduring of the vilification of millions of northern Ivoirians (part of his heritage) and having to prove his own citizenship through the court system (he was declared a citizen by an Ivoirian judge on June 30, 2002, see Skogseth 2006), adds to the interesting dimension of the desire to see whether his lived experience will continue to drive a robust civil and democratic society that opens access to everyone, and adds to the examples of African nations choosing this option.

It is useful to mention in conclusion that despite challenging crises before and during the presidential conflict, Côte d'Ivoire has somewhat stabilized under President Ouattara. It is quite understandable that a couple of years in office are not immediately enough to magically produce change to conditions wrought by decades of crises. However, Ouattara—an economist with multiple international connections—appears to understand that all Ivoirians are to be offered equal opportunities and be treated with respect and dignity as equally deserving citizens. He appears to be appreciated within Côte d'Ivoire and across the globe as his tenure has guided the nation into a robust economic recovery. He was reelected to continue as president of Côte d'Ivoire in 2015 with a whopping approximate 84 percent of the votes (De Rothschild 2015). His economic, political, and social directions appear to anchor the trust and confidence he enjoys from most Ivoirians. If in the past, and despite ethnic differences, Ivoirians were somewhat held together by the first president, Houphouët-Boigny, then it is possible that Ivoirians with President Ouattara's leadership could build on "strength in diversity" to positively redefine Côte d'Ivoire and its national character and future.

References

Acemoglu, Daron, and James A. Robinson. 2006. *Economic Origins of Dictatorship and Democracy*. Cambridge, England: Cambridge University Press.

Adedeji, Adebayo. 1999. *Comprehending and Mastering African Conflicts*. London: Zed Books.

Adon, Gnagui. 2009. *Introduction au Droit de l'Environnement en Afrique: La Cas de la Côte-d'Ivoire*. Paris: Harmattan.

Agou, Waga. 2010. *Gbagbo et-ou le Gâchis Ivoirien*. Paris: Edilivre.

Aka, Bédia F. 2006. *Poverty, Inequality, and Welfare Effects of Trade Liberalization in Côte d'Ivoire: A Computable General Equilibrium Model Analysis*. Nairobi: African Economic Research Consortium.

Akindès, Francis. 2003. "Côte d'Ivoire: Socio-Political Crises, 'Ivoirité,' and the Course of History." *African Sociological Review* 7 (2): 11–28. http://www.jstor.org/stable/43657700.

Alexander, Michelle. 2010. *The New Jim Crow: Mass Incarceration in the Age of Colorblindness*. New York: The New Press.

Allen, Karen. 2011. "Tensions Simmer along Ivory Coast Border Zone." *BBC News*, January 17. http://www.bbc.co.uk/news/world-africa-12210205.

Allport, Gordon Willard. 1954. *The Nature of Prejudice*. Cambridge, MA: Addison-Wesley Publishing Company.

Amnesty International. 2011. "'We Want to Go Home but We Can't': Côte d'Ivoire's Continuing Crisis of Displacement and Insecurity." Report AFR 31/007/2011. Accessed May 29, 2017. https://www.amnesty.org/en/documents/AFR31/007/2011/en/.

Amondji, Marcel. 1986. *Côte-d'Ivoire: Le P.D.C.I. et la Vie Politique de 1944 à 1985*. Paris: L'Harmattan.

Anouma, René-Pierre. 2005. *Aux Origines de la Nation Ivoirienne, 1893–1946*. Paris: Harmattan.

Araoye, Lasisi Ademola. 2012. *Côte d'Ivoire: The Conundrum of a Still Wretched of the Earth.* Trenton, NJ: Africa World Press.

Arthur, Peter. 2010. "ECOWAS and Regional Peacekeeping Integration in West Africa: Lessons for the Future." *Africa Today* 57 (2): 3–24. https://muse.jhu.edu/article/421101.

Assalé, Philippe. 2009. *Les Dessous de la Crise Ivoirienne: D'Houphouët à Guéï*. Paris: L'Harmattan.

Assié-Lumumba, N'Dri Thérèse. 1996. *Les Africaines dans la Politique: Femmes Baoulé de Côte d'Ivoire*. Paris: Éd. l'Harmattan.

Assouman, Kouadio A. 2006. *Le rôle des Nations Unies dans la Resolution de la Crise Ivoirienne*. Abidjan: Centre National de Documentation Juridique.

Attébi, Dadié. 2011. *Du Miracle Économique à la Crise Politique en Côte d'Ivoire*. Paris: L'Harmattan.

Ayittey, George B. N. 1992. *Africa Betrayed*. New York: St. Martin's Press.

———. 2011. *Defeating Dictators: Fighting Tyranny in Africa and Around the World*. New York: Palgrave Macmillan.

Ba, Cheikh Koureyssi, and Mamadou Wade. 2005. *Laurent Gbagbo: C'est le plus Difficile qui est le Chemin*. Abidjan: Le Refondation.

Ba, Oumar. 2016. "Who is Laurent Gbagbo, and Why is He on Trial at the ICC?" 2016. *The Washington Post*, February 3. https://www.washingtonpost.com/news/monkey-cage/wp/2016/02/03/who-is-laurent-gbagbo-and-why-is-he-on-trial-at-the-icc/?utm_term=.1a2ec9e08ae2.

Bah, Abu Bakarr. 2010. "Democracy and Civil War: Citizenship and Peacemaking in Côte d'Ivoire." *African Affairs* 109 (437): 597–615. https://doi.org/10.1093/afraf/adq046.

Bailly, Séry. 2009. *Écrits pour la Démocratie: La Roue Tourne; Essais*. Abidjan: CERAP.

Bally, Edward. 2011. "UNICEF Provides Vital Assistance to Thousands of Displaced People in Côte d'Ivoire." Newsline, May 9. Accessed May 29, 2017. http://www.unicef.org/infobycountry/cotedivoire_58475.html.

Bamba, Kassimi, and Kevin Adou, eds. 2008. *Côte d'Ivoire: Chronique d'une Crise, 2002–2008*. Abidjan: Éditions du CERAP.

Banégas, Richard. 2006. "Côte d'Ivoire: Patriotism, Ethnonationalism and Other African Modes of Self-Writing." *African Affairs* 105 (421): 535–52. https://doi.org/10.1093/afraf/adl035.

Barry, Brian. 2005. *Why Social Justice Matters*. Cambridge, UK: Polity.

Baudrillard, Jean. 1979. *Le Miroir de la Production: Ou, l'Illusion Critique du Matérialisme Historique*. Paris: Casterman.

Baulin, Jacques. 2000. *La Succession d'Houphouët-Boigny: Les Débuts de Konan Bédié*. Paris: Karthala.

Bauman, Zygmunt. 1998. *Globalization: The Human Consequences*. New York: Columbia University Press.

Bellamy, Alex J., and Paul D. Williams. 2011. "The New Politics of Protection? Côte d'Ivoire, Libya and the Responsibility to Protect." *International Affairs* 87 (4): 825–50. doi:10.1111/j.1468-2346.2011.01006.x.

Benjamin, Russell, and Gregory Otha Hall, eds. 2010. *Eternal Colonialism*. Lanham, MD: University Press of America.

Besnahan, Robyn. 2011. "Ivory Coast politics ruined my marriage." *BBC News*, October 19. http://www.bbc.co.uk/news/world-africa-15350599.

Bhagwati, Jagdish N. 2004. *In Defense of Globalization*. New York: Oxford University Press.

Biko, Steve, and Aelred Stubbs. 1978. *I Write What I Like: A Selection of His Writings Edited with a Personal Memoir*. New York: Harper and Row.

Blé Goudé, Charles. 2006. *Ma Part de Vérité*. 2nd ed. Abidjan: Leaders Team.

Bond, Patrick. 2006. *Looting Africa: The Economics of Exploitation*. Pietermaritzburg: University of Kwazulu Natal Press.

Bosson, Brou Evariste. 1994. *Sur la Route des Temps Nouveaux Avec Henri Konan Bédié*. Abidjan: Editions Akohi.

Brown, Graham K., and Arnim Langer. 2010. "Horizontal Inequalities and Conflict: A Critical Review and Research Agenda." *Conflict, Security, and Development* 10 (1): 27–55. http://dx.doi.org/10.1080/14678800903553837.

Burggraeve, Roger. 1985. *From Self-Development to Solidarity: An Ethical Reading of Human Desire in its Socio-political Relevance According to Emmanuel Levinas*. Leuven, Belgium: Peeters.

Bush, Robert A. Baruch, and Joseph P. Folger. 2005. *The Promise of Mediation: The Transformative Approach to Conflict*. rev. ed. San Francisco: Jossey-Bass.

Butty, James. 2011. "ECOWAS Leaders Return to Ivory Coast Monday not to Negotiate." *Voice of America*, January 2. http://www.voanews.com/english/news/ africa/Butty-Ivory-Coast-ECOWAS-Round-2-Kargbo-03january10-112790454.html.

Byrne, Sean, and Neal Carter. 1996. "Social Cubism: Six Social Forces of Ethnoterritorial Politics in Northern Ireland and Québec." *Peace and Conflict Studies* 3 (2): 52–71. http://nsuworks.nova.edu/pcs/vol3/iss2/5/.

Byrne, Sean, Neal Carter, and Jessica Senehi. 2002. "Social Cubism and Social Conflict: Analysis and Resolution." *ILSA Journal of International & Comparative Law* 8 (3): 725–40. http://nsuworks.nova.edu/ilsajournal/vol8/iss3/1/.

Canagarajah, Sudharshan, and Helena Skyt Nielsen. 2001. "Child Labor and Schooling in Africa: A Comparative Study." *ANNALS of the American Academy of Political and Social Science* 575 (1): 71–91. https://doi.org/10.1177/000271620157500105.

Carmichael, Stokely, and Charles V. Hamilton. 1967. *Black Power: The Politics of Liberation in America*. New York: Random House.

Carver, John. 2002. *John Carver on Board Leadership: Selected Writings from the Creator of the World's Most Provocative and Systematic Governance Model*. San Francisco: Jossey-Bass.

Central Intelligence Agency. 2017. "Cote d'Ivoire." In *The World Fact Book*. https://www.cia.gov/library/publications/the-world-factbook/geos/iv.html.

Centre Ivoirien de Recherche Économique et Sociale (CIRES). 2008. *Democratie, Droit de l'Homme, Bonne Gouvernance et Developpement*. Abidjan: Éditions Universitaires de Côte d'Ivoire.

Charrad, M. Mourina. 2001. *States and Women's Rights: The Making of Postcolonial Tunisia, Algeria, and Morocco*. Berkeley: University of California Press.

Charvin, Robert. 2011. *Côte d'Ivoire 2011: La Bataille de la Seconde Indépendance*. Paris: Harmattan.

"Chinua Achebe Award Snub 'Surprises' Nigerian President." 2011. *BBC News*, November 14. http://www.bbc.com/news/world-africa-15720476.

Chirot, Daniel. 2006. "The Debacle in Côte d'Ivoire." *Journal of Democracy* 17 (2): 63–77. https://doi.org/10.1353/jod.2006.0024.

Chomsky, Noam. 2011. "Noam Chomsky: 'As long they get the backing of dictators, it doesn't matter to western governments what Arab populations think'—video" (video commentary). *The Guardian*, August 31. Accessed May 29, 2017. http://www.guardian.co.uk/commentisfree/video/2011/aug/31/noam-chomsky-terrorism-video.

Chomsky, Noam. 2017. *Requiem for the American Dream: The Principles of Concentrated Wealth and Power*. New York: Seven Stories Press.

Cissé, Ibrahim Bacongo. 2007. *Alassane Dramane Ouattara: Histoire d'une vie Singulière: Légende et Épopée*. Abidjan, Côte d'Ivoire: NEI/CEDA.

Colin, Jean-Phillipe, Georges Kouamé, and Debegnoun Soro. 2007. "Outside the Autochthon—Migrant Configuration: Access to Land, Land Conflicts and Inter-Ethnic Relationships in a Former Pioneer are of Flower Côte d'Ivoire." *Journal of Modern African Studies* 45 (1): 33–59.

Collett, Moya. 2006. "Ivoirian Identity Constructions: Ethnicity and Nationalism in the Prelude to Civil War." *Nations and Nationalism* 12 (4): 613–29. doi:10.1111/j.1469-8129.2006.00260.x.

Comim, Flavio, Mozaffar Qizilbash, and Sabina Alkire. 2008. *The Capability Approach: Concepts, Measures and Applications*. New York: Cambridge University Press.

Cone, James. H. 1969. *Black Theology and Black Power*. New York: Seabury Press.

———. 1970. *A Black Theology of Liberation*. Philadelphia: Lippincott.

Cooper, Helene. 2017. *Madame President: The Extraordinary Journey of Ellen Johnson Sirleaf.* New York: Simon & Schuster.

Copnall, James. 2004. "Ivory Coast's Cultural Divide." *BBC News*, July 17. http://news.bbc.co.uk/2/hi/africa/3901939.stm.

Côte d'Ivoire, and Food and Agriculture Organization of the United Nations. 2008. *Les Bilans Alimentaires de la Côte d'Ivoire, 2001–2007 (Juin 2008)*. Abidjan: Republique de Côte d'Ivoire, Ministere de l'Agriculture, Direction des Statistiques, de la Documentation et de l'Informatique.

"Côte d'Ivoire: Gbagbo Surrenders." 2011. *Africa Research Bulletin* 48 (3): 1–2. doi:10.1111/j.1467-6346.2011.03817.x.

Coulibaly, Djakalidja. 2011. *Agriculture et Protection de l'Environnement dans le Sud-ouest de la Côte d'Ivoire: Entre Logiques Marchandes et Logiques Écologiques*. Paris: L'Harmattan.

Dahrendorf, Ralf. 1959. *Class and Class Conflict in Industrial Society*. Stanford: Stanford University Press.

Danziger, Danny, and John Gillingham. 2004. *1215: The Year of Magna Carta*. New York: Simon & Schuster.

Davis, Kingsley, and Wilbert E. Moore. 1945. *Some Principles of Stratification*. Indianapolis: Bobbs-Merrill.

Dean, Thalif. 2011. "UNICEF Leads 'Back to School' Initiative in Côte d'Ivoire." *Inter Press Service (IPS)*, June 28. http://www.ipsnews.net/2011/06/unicef-leads-back-to-school-initiative-in-cote-divoire/.

De Leon, Daniel. 1886. "The Conference at Berlin on the West-African Question." *Political Science Quarterly* 1 (1): 103–39. http://www.jstor.org/stable/2139304.

Deleuze, Gilles, and Félix Guattari. 1972. *Capitalisme et Schizophrénie*. Paris: Editions de Minui.

De Rothschild, Saskia. 2015. "Alassane Ouattara Is Re-elected President of Ivory Coast." The *New York Times*, October 28. https://www.nytimes.com/2015/10/29/world/africa/alassane-ouattara-is-re-elected-president-of-ivory-coast.html?_r=0.

Dinan, Stephen. 2009. "Obama to African Leaders: Time for 'Responsibility.'" The *Washington Times*, July 11. Accessed May 28, 2017. http://www.washingtontimes.com/news/2009/jul/11/obama-to-africas-leaders-time-for-responsibility/.

Diop, Cheikh Anta. 1974. *The African Origin of Civilization: Myth or Realty*. Translated by Mercer Cook. New York: Lawrence Hill Books.

———. 1987. *Precolonial Black Africa: A Comparative Study of the Political and Social Systems of Europe and Black Africa, from Antiquity to the Formation of Modern States*. Translated by Harold J. Salemson. New York: Lawrence Hill Books.

Djea, Jean-Luc. 2009. *Histoire Récente de la Côte d'Ivoire: Le Sphinx au Porte de Palaise*. Abidjan: Sesamé Édition.

Doise, Willem. 1978. *Groups and Individuals: Explanations in Social Psychology*. Cambridge: Cambridge University Press.

Doukoure, Lassiné. 2002. *Analyse de la Pauvreté Alimentaire en Côte d'Ivoire*. [Abidjan?]: Institut National de la Statistique.

Doyle, Mark. 2011. "The Politics of Human Rights in Ivory Coast." *BBC News*, May 25. http://www.bbc.co.uk/news/world-africa-13528781.

D'Souza, Dinesh. 1995. *The End of Racism: Principles for a Multiracial Society*. New York: Free Press.

Duhy, Ernest. 2006. *Le Pouvoir est un Service: Ce Cas Laurent Gbagbo*. Paris: L'Harmattan.

Dumas, Roland, and Jacques Vergès. 2011. *Crimes et Frauds en Côte-d'Ivoire*. Paris: Edite.

Dussel, Enrique D. 1978. *Ethics and the Theology of Liberation*. Translated by Bernard F. McWilliams. Maryknoll, NY: Orbis Books.

———. 1979. *El Episcopado Latinoamericano y la Liberación de los Pobres, 1504-1620*. México: Centro de Reflexión Teológica.

———. 1980. *Filosofía de la Liberación*. Bogotá: Universidad Santo Tomás, Centro de Enseñanza Desescolarizada.

Dutheuill, Gisèle. 2008. *À l'Intelligentsia Ivoirienne: Oser une Nouvelle Voie*. Paris: L'Harmattan.

Ehusani, George Omaku. 2002. *Nigeria: Years Eaten by the Locust*. Ibadan, Nigeria: Kraft Books.

Eichstaedt, Peter. 2010. *Pirate State: Inside Somalia's Terrorism at Sea*. Chicago: Lawrence Hill Books.

Ekanza, Simon-Pierre. 2007. *Côte-d'Ivoire: De l'Ethnie à la Nation, une Histoire à Bâtir*. Abidjan: Éditions du CERAP.

Ellacuría, Ignacio. 1980. *Fe, Justicia y Opción por los Oprimidos*. Bilbao: Desclée de Brouwer, D.L.

———. 1987. *El Salvador: Crisis Económica*. México: Centro de Investigación y Acción Social.

———. 1989. *Implicaciones Sociales y Políticas de la Teología de la Liberación*. Sevilla: Escuela de Estudios Hispanoamericanos, Instituto de Filosofia.
Ellacuría, Ignacio, and Jon Sobrino, eds. 1990. 1. *Mysterium Liberationis: Fundamental Concepts of Liberation Theology*. Maryknoll, NY: Orbis Books.
Emeagwali, Philip. 2003. "How Do We Reverse the Brain Drain?" Keynote speech at the Pan African Conference on Brain Drain, Elsah, Illinois, October 24. Accessed May 29, 2017. http://emeagwali.com/speeches/brain-drain/to-brain-gain/reverse-brain-drain-from-africa.html.
Falola, Tolin, and Matthew M. Heaton. 2008. *A History of Nigeria*. Cambridge: Cambridge University Press.
Fanon, Frantz. 1965. *The Wretched of the Earth*. New York: Grove Press.
Fauré, Yves. 1993. "Democracy and Realism: Reflections on the Case of Côte d'Ivoire." *Africa: Journal of the International African Institute* 63(3): 313–29. https://doi.org/10.2307/1161425.
Fiorenza, Elisabeth Schussler. 1983. *In Memory of Her: A Feminist Theological Reconstruction of Christian Origins*. New York: Crossroad.
Fofana, Lémassou. 2007. *Côte-d'Ivoire: Islam et Sociétés: Contribution des Musulmans à l'Édification de la Nation Ivoirienne (XIe-XXe Siècles)*. Abidjan: Editions du CERAP.
Folger, Joseph P., Marshall Scott Poole, and Randall K. Stutman. 2005. *Working through Conflict: Strategies for Relationships, Groups, and Organizations*. 5th ed. Boston: Pearson.
Fonds Africain de Developpement. 1997. *République de Côte d'Ivoire, Projet d'Appui au Développement Rural de la Région Centre: Rapport d'Evaluation*. Abidjan: Fonds Africain de Développement.
Forsyth, Christopher, Mark Elliott, Swati Jhaveri, Anne Scully-Hill, and Michael Ramsden, eds. 2010. *Effective Judicial Review: A Cornerstone of Good Governance*. Oxford: Oxford University Press.
Foucault, Michel. 1977. *Discipline and Punish: The Birth of the Prison*. 1st ed. Translated by Alan M. Sheridan Smith. New York: Pantheon Books.
———. 2002. *Archaeology of Knowledge*. Translated by Alan M. Sheridan Smith. London: Routledge.
Freire, Paulo. 1990. *Pedagogy of the Oppressed*. Translated by Myra Bergman Ramos. New York: Continuum.
Front Populair Ivoireine. 1987. *Proposition pour Gouverner Côte d'Ivoire*. Paris: L'Harmattan.
Gakunzi, David. 2011. *Côte d'Ivoire, le Crime Parfait*. Paris: L'Harmattan.
Galtung, Johan. 1971. "A Structural Theory of Imperialism." *Journal of Peace Research* 8 (2): 81–117. http://www.jstor.org/stable/422946.
Gazoa, Germain. 2006. *Les Conflits en Afrique Noire: Quelles Solutions? Approches Spirituelles et Anthropologiques: Le Cas Ivoirien*. Abidjan: Frat Mat Éditions.
Gbagbo, Laurent. 1982. *La Côte-d'Ivoire: Économie et Société à la Veille de l'Indépendance, 1940-1960*. Paris: L'Harmattan.
———. 1983. *Côte-d'Ivoire: Pour une Alternative Démocratique*. Paris: L'Harmattan.
———. 1989. *Côte-d'Ivoire: Histoire d'un Retour*. Paris: L'Harmattan.
———. 1991. *Côte d'Ivoire: Agir pour les Libertés*. Paris: L'Harmattan.
———. 2009. *Côte d'Ivoire: Bâtir la Paix sur la Démocratie et la Prosperité*. Abidjan: NEI-CEDA.
Gbagbo, Laurent, and Honoré De Sumo. 1995. *Le temps de l'Espoir: Entretiens avec Honoré De Sumo*. Johannesburg: Editions Continentales.
Gbagbo, Michel. 2006. *Côte d'Ivoire: Un Air de Changement*. Abidjan: CEDA/NEI.
Gilligan, Carol. 1982. *In a Different Voice: Psychological Theory and Women's Development*. Cambridge, MA: Harvard University Press.
Goba, Arsène Ouegui. 2000. *Côte-d'Ivoire—Quelle Issue pour la Transition?* Paris: Harmattan.
Godwin, Peter. 2011. *The Fear: Robert Mugabe and the Martyrdom of Zimbabwe*. New York: Little, Brown and Co.
Gonnin, Gilbert. 2006. *Côte-d'Ivoire: Les Premiers Habitants*. Abidjan: CERAP.
Greene, Robert. 2000. *The 48 Laws of Power*. New York: Penguin.

Grootaert, Christiaan, Lionel Demery, and S. M. Ravi Kankur. 1996. *Analyzing Poverty and Policy Reform: The Experience of Côte d'Ivoire*. Aldershot: Avebury Press.

Guattari, Félix. 1995. *Chaosmosis: An Ethico-Aesthetic Paradigm*. Bloomington: University of Indiana Press.

Gutiérrez, Gustavo. 1973. *A Theology of Liberation: History, Politics, and Salvation*. Translated by S. Caridad Inda and John Eagleson. Maryknoll, NY: Orbis Books.

Hamilton, Rebecca. 2011. *Fighting for Darfur: Public Action and the Struggle to Stop Genocide*. New York: Palgrave Macmillan.

Herrnstein, Richard J., and Charles A. Murray. 1994. *Bell Curve: Intelligence and Class Structure in America* . New York: Free Press.

Holy, Bedi. 2006. *Ils ont Failli Assassiner la Fraternité*. Abidjan: Editions du défi.

Horkheimer, Max. 1972. *Critical Theory, Selected Essays*. Translated by Matthew J. O'Connell. New York: Herder and Herder.

Hume, David. 1934. *A Treatise of Human Nature*. London: J.M. Dent & Sons Ltd.

International Criminal Court. 2011. "Confirmation of Charges Hearing in the Case of *The Prosecutor v. Laurent Koudou Gbagbo* Scheduled to Start on 18 June 2012." *ICC Weekly Update* 107, December 12. https://www.icc-cpi.int/NR/rdonlyres/D391FDC2-6326-4068-B048-6908D258D38A/284090/Ed107Eng.pdf.

International Crisis Group. 2004. "Côte d'Ivoire: No Peace in Sight." Report no. 82. http://cms.crisisgroup.org/africa/west-africa/c%C3%B4te-divoire/cote-divoire-no-peace-sight.

Ikome, Francis Nguendi, Siphamandla Zondi, and Venance Konan, eds. 2006. *La Côte d'Ivoire: Vers une Transition Politique Pacifique, un Pays Unifié et un Avenir Prospère: Synthèse et Analyses de la Table Ronde Tenu à Grand Bassam, Côte d'Ivoire, les 9, 10 et 11 Novembre 2005*. Midrand, South Africa: Institute for Global Dialogue.

IRIN. 2005. "Thousands of Migrants Now Living as Strangers in their Homeland." Report, February 18. http://www.irinnews.org/feature/2005/02/18/thousands-migrants-now-living-strangers-their-homeland.

———. 2011. "Unrest disrupts malaria prevention bid." Report, June 7. http://www.irinnews.org/Report/92926/COTE-D-IVOIRE-Unrest-disrupts-malaria-prevention-bid.

———. 2012. "Leprosy Flight Still Flagging." Report, February 8. http://www.irinnews.org/Report/94814/COTE-D-IVOIRE-Leprosy-fight-still-flagging.

Ismail, Olawale. 2008. "Power Elites, War and Postwar Reconstruction in Africa: Continuities, Discontinuities and Paradoxes." *Journal of Contemporary African Studies* 26 (3): 259–78. http://dx.doi.org/10.1080/02589000802332457.

"Ivory Coast Conflict: Gbagbo Ally Jailed over Novotel Hotel Murders." 2017. *BBC News*, April 14. http://www.bbc.com/news/world-africa-39599099.

"Ivory Coast Poll Overturned: Gbagbo Declared Winner." 2010. *BBC News*, December 3. http://www.bbc.co.uk/news/world-africa-11913832.

"Ivory Coast: Pre-European Period." 1988. In *Encyclopedia of Nations*. http://www.country-data.com/cgi-bin/query/r-6886.html.

"Ivory Coast's former first lady Simone Gbagbo jailed." 2015. *BBC News*, March 10. http://www.bbc.com/news/world-africa-31809073.

Jaboro, Majemite. 2012. *The Ikoyi Prison Narratives: The Spiritualism and Political Philosophy of Fela Kuti*. Online: lulu.com.

James, John. 2010. "Ivory Coast: Two Presidents, One Crisis." *BBC News*, December 8. http://www.bbc.co.uk/news/world-africa-11939113.

Jameson, Fredric. 1991. *Postmodernism, or the Cultural Logic of Late Capitalism*. Durham, NC: Duke University Press.

Jeong, Ho-Won. 2000. *Peace and Conflict Studies: An Introduction*. Aldershot: Ashgate.

Kaba, Amadu Jacky. 2004. "Africa's Migration Brain Drain: The Costs and Benefits to the Continent." *Chimera* 2 (3): 19–30. https://works.bepress.com/amadu_kaba/30/.

———. 2005. "Africa's Migration and Terminal Brain Drain." *African Renaissance* 2 (4): 111–18.

Kakwani, Nanak. 1990. *Poverty and Economic Growth: With Application to Côte d'Ivoire*. Washington, DC: World Bank.

Karenga, Maulana. 2002. *Introduction to Black Studies*. Los Angeles: University of Sankore Press.
King, Jr., Martin Luther. 1958. *Stride toward Freedom: The Montgomery Story*. New York: Harper.
Klaas, Brian. 2008. "From Miracle to Nightmare: An Institutional Analysis of Development Failures in Côte d'Ivoire." *Africa Today* 55 (1): 109–126. https://muse.jhu.edu/article/250682.
Koffi, Paul Koffi. 2008. *Le Défi du Développement en Côte d'Ivoire*. Paris: L'Harmattan.
———. 2010. *Houphouët et les Mutations Politiques en Côte d'Ivoire: 1980-1993*. Paris: Harmattan.
Koffi, Tiburce. 2006. *Côte d'Ivoire, l'Agonie du Jardin : Du Grand Rêve au Désastre*. Abidjan: CEDA/NEI.
Konaté, Siendou A. 2005. "The Politics of Identity and Violence in Côte d'Ivoire." *The Patriotic Guard: Sierra Leone News Portal*, August 1. http://www.thepatrioticvanguard.com/article.php3?id_article=91.
Koné, Mariatou. 2005. *Socio-Anthropologie de la Famille en Afrique: Évolution des Modèles en Côte d'Ivoire*. Abidjan: Éditions du CERAP.
Kotoudi, Idimama. 2004. *Comprendre et Traiter la Crise en Côte d'Ivoire*. Dakar: Institut Panos Afrique de l'Ouest.
Kouadio, Bertin K. 2009. "From Stability to Insurgency: The Root and Proximate Causes of the September 2002 Civil War in Côte d'Ivoire." PhD diss., Florida International University, Miami. http://digitalcommons.fiu.edu/etd/115.
Kouadio, Boni. 2006. *Discours sur l'Impérialisme*. Abidjan-Riviera: PUCI.
Kouamouo, Théophile. 2007. *La Recolonisation de l'Afrique: Le Cas de la Côte d'Ivoire*. Abidjan: Editions Le Courrier.
Koudou, Claude, ed. 2006. *L'espérance en Côte d'Ivoire: Colloque International sur la Côte d'Ivoire*. Paris: Harmattan.
Koui, Théophile. 2010. *Côte d'Ivoire: Les Cavaliers de l'Apocalypse*. Paris: L'Harmattan.
Koulibaly, Mamadou. 2004. *Sur la Route de la Liberté*. Paris: L'Harmattan.
———. 2009. *Eurafrique ou Librafrique: l'ONU et les Non-Dits du Pacte Colonial*. Paris: L'Harmattan.
Langer, Arnim. 2005. "Horizontal Inequalities and Violent Group Mobilization in Côte d'Ivoire." *Oxford Development Studies* 33 (1): 25–45. http://dx.doi.org/10.1080/13600810500099634.
Le Patriote. 2011. "Après le Second Tour des Élections de 2010 Nous Avons Deux Résultats." *Abidjan.net*, January 14. http://news.abidjan.net/h/387323.html.
Lutuli, Albert John. 1962. *Let My People Go: An Autobiography*. Johannesburg: Collins.
Lyotard, Jean-François. 1979. *La Condition Postmoderne: Rapport sur le Savoir*. Paris: Éditions de Minuit.
Macguire, Eoghan. 2011. "Ivory Coast Seeks Chocolate Fairness for Farmers." *CNN*, November 25. http://edition.cnn.com/2011/11/25/business/mpa-ivory-coast-cocoa/index.html.
MacIntyre, Alasdair C. 1981. *After Virtue: A Study in Moral Theory*. Notre Dame, IN: University of Notre Dame Press.
———. 1988. *Whose Justice? Which Rationality?* Notre Dame, IN: University of Notre Dame Press.
Marx, Karl. 1934. *Capital: A Critique of Political Economy*. London: J.M. Dent & Sons Ltd.
Mazrui, Ali A., ed. 1999. *General History of Africa: Volume VIII: Africa since 1935*. Berkeley: University of California Press.
Mbamara, Oliver. 2009. "Responsibility and Accountability from the Top: The Kind of Rebranding We Need." *Nigerians in America*, September 8. http://www.africanevents.com/Essay-AccountabilityResponsibilityWeNeed-Pt2.htm.
Mbeki, Thabo. 2011. "What the World Got Wrong in Côte d'Ivoire." *Foreign Policy*, April 29. http://foreignpolicy.com/2011/04/29/what-the-world-got-wrong-in-cote-divoire/.
Mbem, André Julien. 2010. *Laurent Gbagbo: L'intellectuel et le Politique*. Paris: L'Harmattan.
McCann, Carole R., and Kim Seung-Kyung, eds. 2010. *Feminist Theory Reader: Local and Global Perspectives*. 2nd ed. New York: Routledge.

McCauley, John F. 2017. *The Logic of Ethnic and Religious Conflict in Africa*. New York: Cambridge University Press.

McGovern, Mike. 2011. *Making War in Côte d'Ivoire*. Chicago: University of Chicago Press.

McKay, Judith. 2002. "The Use of Social Cubism in the Analysis of Community Conflicts." *ILSA Journal of International & Comparative Law* 8 (3): 883–900. http://nsuworks.nova.edu/cgi/viewcontent.cgi?article=1391&context=ilsajournal.

Meehan, Patrick. 2011. "The 'Problem' with Côte d'Ivoire: How the Media Misrepresent the Causes of Conflict." *Open Security*, January 13. https://www.opendemocracy.net/opensecurity/patrick-meehan/problem-with-c%c3%b4te-d%e2%80%99ivoire-how-media-misrepresent-causes-of-conflict.

Mel, Frédéric Grah. 2005. *Rencontres avec Félix Houphouët-Boigny*. Abidjan: Frat Mat Éditions.

Mills, C. Wright. 1951. *White Collar: The American Middle Classes*. New York: Oxford University Press.

———. 1956. *Power Elite*. New York: Oxford University Press.

Moon, Bob. 2008. "Banks Deep into Unregulated Gambling." *American Public Media: Marketplace*, April 1. http://www.marketplace.org/topics/your-money/banks-deep-unregulated-gambling.

Moore, Barrington. 1966. *Social Origins of Dictatorship and Democracy: Lord and Peasant in the Making of the Modern World*. Boston: Beacon Press.

Moore, Basil, ed. 1973. *Black Theology: The South African Voice*. London: C. Hurst.

Moore, Christopher W. 2003. *The Mediation Process: Practical Strategies for Resolving Conflicts*. San Francisco: Jossey-Bass.

Morel, Colombre. 2006. *La Vérité sur la Guerre en Côte d'Ivoire et les Intérêts Politiques*. Paris: Publieur.

Moyers, Bill. 2003. "Rich World, Poor Women" [Television broadcast transcript]. In *PBS Now*, produced by Bill Moyers, September 5. http://www.pbs.org/now/transcript/transcript233_full.html

Moyo, Dambisa. 2009. *Dead Aid: Why Aid is not Working and How There is a Better Way for Africa*. New York: Farrar, Straus, & Giroux.

Mudimbe, Valentine Y., ed. 1992. *The Surreptitious Speech: Présence Africaine and the Politics of Otherness, 1947–1987*. Chicago: University of Chicago Press.

Mudimbe-Boyi, Elisabeth, ed. 2009. *Empire Lost: France and its Other Worlds*. Lanham, MD: Lexington Books.

Nation Correspondent. 1998. "Kenya: Prof. Ali Mazrui Hits at Corrupt Kenya." *allAfrica.com*, December 7. http://allafrica.com/stories/199812070067.html.

Nathanson, Stephen. 1998. *Economic Justice*. Upper Saddle River, NJ: Prentice Hall.

Ndiaye, Malick. 2011. *Où va la Côte d'Ivoire? Entre la Question Juula, le Complexe d'Akan et le Souverainisme de Laurent Gbagbo*. Paris: Harmattan.

Ndlovu-Gatsheni, Sabelo J. 2010. "Do 'Africans' Exist? Genealogies and Paradoxes of African Identities and the Discourses of Nativism and Xenophobia." *African Identities* 8 (3): 281–95. http://dx.doi.org/10.1080/14725843.2010.491972.

Nhema, Alfred G., ed. 2004. *The Quest for Peace in Africa: Transformation, Democracy, and Public Policy*. Addis Ababa, Ethiopia: OSSREA & Utrecht, International Books.

Nicholson, Linda J. 1999. *The Play of Reason: From the Modern to the Postmodern*. Buckingham: Open University Press.

Nkwocha, Onyema. 2010. *Republic of Biafra: Once Upon a Time in Nigeria: My Story of the Biafran-Nigerian Civil War—A Struggle for Survival (1967–1970)*. Bloomington, IN: Authorhouse.

Novak, Michael. 2000. "Defining Social Justice." *First Things*, December. Accessed May 28, 2017. https://www.firstthings.com/article/2000/12/defining-social-justice.

Novak, Michael, and Paul Adams. 2015. *Social Justice Isn't What You Think It Is*. New York: Encounter Books.

Nussbaum, Martha Craven. 2011. *Creating Capabilities: The Human Development Approach*. Cambridge, MA: Belknap Press of Harvard University Press.

Nyerere, Julius K. 1968. *Freedom and Socialism = Uhuru na ujamaa: A Selection from Writings and Speeches, 1965–1967*. New York: Oxford University Press.

Obou, Thibeaud. 2009. *Bâtir la Côte d'Ivoire*. 2nd ed. Deuil-la-Barre: Akofa-Bisola.

Okon, Guy Michel. 2002. *Enquete Niveau de vie des Menages Côte d'Ivoire 2002: Education et Pauvrete en Côte d'Ivoire*. With assistance from Adjoba Yvette Essouin. Abidjan: Institut national de la statistique, Republique de Côte d'Ivoire.

Okosun, T. Y. 2010. "Africa in Fragments: Justice, Politics, and Transformation." In *Eternal Colonialism*, edited by Russell Benjamin and Gregory Otha Hall, 147–68. Lanham, MD: University Press of America.

———. 2009. *Social Justice and Increasing Global Destitution*. Lanham, MD: University Press of America.

Okosun, T. Y., and Naupess Kibiswa. 2013. "Human Rights Violations and Genocide in the Democratic Republic of the Congo." *Contemporary Justice Review* 16 (4): 482—93. http://dx.doi.org/10.1080/10282580.2013.857074.

Olaniyan, Tejumola. 2004. *Arrest the Music! Fela and His Rebel Art and Politics*. Bloomington, IN: Indiana University Press.

Oloruntimehin, B. Olatunji. 1993. "French Colonisation and African Resistance in West Africa Up to the First World War." In *Conquest and Resistance to Colonialism in Africa*, edited by Gregory Maddox, 102–112. New York: Garland.

O'Sullivan, John M. 1993. "The Franco-Baoule War, 1891–1911: The Struggle Against the French Conquest of Central Ivory Coast." In *Conquest and Resistance to Colonialism in Africa*, edited by Gregory Maddox, 73–100. New York: Garland.

Ott, Thomas O. 1987. *The Haitian Revolution, 1789–1804*. Knoxville, TN: University of Tennessee Press.

Ottemey, Nane Tory. 2009. *L'amitié Coupable: De la Françafrique à la Francivoire, L'illusion d'une Idylle Coloniale*. Paris: Menaibuc.

Ouattara, Idrissa. 2003. *Profil de Pauvreté en Côte d'Ivoire en 2002: Résultats Provisoires*. Abidjan: Institut National de la Statistique.

Ouédraogo, Jean-Bernard, and Ebrima Sall, eds. 2008. *Frontières de la Citoyenneté et Violence Politique en Côte d'Ivoire*. Dakar: Codesria.

Oved, Marco. 2010. "Ivory Coast Closes Land, Air, Sea Borders after Presidential Election: Ivory Coast Opposition Leader Alassane Ouattara Wins Elections: Ruling Party Calls it a Coup." *The Star*, December 2. https://www.thestar.com/news/world/2010/12/02/ivory_coast_closes_land_air_sea_borders_after_presidential_election.html.

Palitza, Kristin. 2012. "The Lost Innocence of Côte d'Ivoire's Children." *IPS Africa*, March 19. http://www.ipsnews.net/2012/03/the-lost-innocence-of-cote-drsquoivoirersquos-children/.

Pawson, Lara. 2004. "Ethnic Split Stirs Ivory Coast's Crisis." *BBC News*, February 18. http://news.bbc.co.uk/2/hi/africa/3496069.stm.

Pruitt, Dean G., and Sung Hee Kim. 2004. *Social Conflict: Escalation, Stalemate, and Settlement*. 3rd ed. Boston: McGraw Hill.

Putnam, Robert D. 2009. "Making Democracy Work." In *The Civil Society Reader*, edited by Virginia Ann Hodgkinson and Michael W. Foley, 322–27. London: Tuft University Press.

"Q&A: Ivory Coast Crisis." 2011. *BBC News*, April 13. http://www.bbc.co.uk/news/world-africa-11916590.

Quenum, Bienvenu-Magloire. 2011a. "Facts to the Political Crisis in Ivory Coast: Henri Konan Bedie Rise to Power." *Africabiz Online*. http://businessafrica.net/africabiz/ezine/wa/newswaf3.php.

———. 2011b. "Facts to Understanding the Post-Electoral Imbroglio in Ivory Coast." *Africabiz Online*. http://businessafrica.net/africabiz/arcvol2/email121.php#imbroglio.

———. 2011c. "Facts to the Political Crisis in Ivory Coast: The Fight for the Presidency between Gbagbo and Ouattara." *Africabiz Online*. http://businessafrica.net/africabiz/ezine/wa/newswaf4.php.

———. 2011d. "Facts to the Political Crisis in Ivory Coast: No Civil War after Gbagbo Downfall." *Africabiz Online*. http://businessafrica.net/africabiz/ezine/wa/newswaf5.php.

Quist-Arcton, Ofeibea. 2011. "Ivory Coast's 'Young Patriots' Volunteer to Fight." *NPR*, March 2011. http://www.npr.org/2011/03/21/134743394/ivory-coasts-young-patriots-volunteer-to-fight.

Rawls, John. 1971. *A Theory of Justice*. Cambridge, MA: Harvard University Press.

———. 2001. *Justice as Fairness: A Restatement*. Cambridge, MA: Harvard University Press.

Ritzer, George, and Douglas J. Goodman. 2004. *Sociological Theory*. Boston: McGraw-Hill.

Robinson, Randall. 2000. *The Debt: What America Owes to Blacks*. New York: Dutton.

Rodney, Walter. 1972. *How Europe Underdeveloped Africa*. Washington, DC: Howard University Press.

Romero, Óscar A. 1981. *A Martyr's Message of Hope: Six Homilies*. Kansas City, MO: Celebration Books.

Ruether, Rosemary Radford. 1983. *Sexism and God-talk: Toward a Feminist Theology*. Boston: Beacon Press.

Rushton, J. Philippe. 1995. *Race, Evolution, and Behavior: A Life History Perspective* . New Brunswick, NJ: Transaction Publishers.

Russell, Jason (Director). 2012a. "Kony 2012, Part I: Invisible Children," (video documentary). Accessed June 2, 2017. https://www.youtube.com/watch?v=Y4MnpzG5Sqc.

Russell, Jason (Director). 2012b. "Kony 2012, Part II: Beyond Famous," (video documentary). Accessed June 2, 2017. https://www.youtube.com/watch?v=c_Ue6REkeTA.

Ruwe, Field. 2012. "You Lazy (Intellectual) African Scum!" *Mind of Malaka*, guest post, January 18. http://mindofmalaka.com/2012/01/18/you-lazy-intellectual-african-scum/#comments.

Sachs, Jeffrey. 2005. *The End of Poverty: Economic Possibilities for Our Time*. New York: Penguin Press.

Sahi, Alphonse Voho. 2005. *Une Chronique de la Révolution Démocratique en Côte d'Ivoire (1989-1995)*. Abidjan, Côte d'Ivoire: Nouvelles éditions Ivoirienne.

Salau, Gbenga. 2017. Mutiny: Signs of Ivory Coast's Fragile Peace. *The Guardian*, May 21. http://guardian.ng/politics/mutiny-signs-of-ivory-coasts-fragile-peace/.

Sandel, Michael J. 2009. *Justice: What's the Right Thing to Do?* New York: Farrar, Straus, and Giroux.

Scheuer, Benoît, and Dominique Trembloy. 2001. "Ivory Coast: The Identity Powder Keg," (video). Accessed June 2, 2017. http://vimeo.com/10313876.

Schellenberg, James A. 1996. *Conflict Resolution: Theory, Research, and Practice*. Albany: State University of New York Press.

Sekularac, Ivana. 2011. "Gbagbo Faces Charges of Crimes against Humanity: ICC." *Reuters*, November 30. http://www.reuters.com/article/2011/11/30/us-ivorycoast-gbagbo-idUSTRE7AT1UP20111130.

Sen, Amartya Kumar. 1992. *Inequality Reexamined*. Cambridge: Harvard University Press.

———. 1999. *Commodities and Capabilities*. New York: Oxford University Press.

———. 2001. *Development as Freedom*. New York: Anchor.

———. 2009. *The Idea of Justice*. Cambridge: Belknap Press of Harvard University Press.

Sen, Gita, and Caren Grown. 1987. *Development, Crises, and Alternative Visions: Third World Women's Perspectives*. New York: Monthly Review Press.

Sewpaul, Vishanthie, and Dorothee Hölscher. 2004. *Social Work in Times of Neoliberalism: A Postmodern Discourse*. Pretoria: Van Schaik Publishers.

Shils, Edward. 2009. "The Virtue of Civil Society." In *The Civil Society Reader*, edited by Virginia Ann Hodgkinson and Michael W. Foley, 292–305. London: Tuft University Press.

Shiner, Cindy. 2010. Côte d'Ivoire: Armed, Masked Men Terrorize West, Says Rights Group. *AllAfrica*, October 22. http://allafrica.com/stories/201010220649.html

Shiva, Vandana. 1993. *Monocultures of the Mind: Perspectives on Biodiversity and Biotechnology*. Atlantic Highlands, NJ: Zed Books.

Shoemaker, Pamela J., James W. Tankard, and Dominic L. Lasorsa. 2004. *How to Build Social Science Theories*. Thousand Oaks, CA: Sage Publications.

Sibi, Aliou, and Henri Konan Bédié. 1995. *Le Pari de l'an 2000: Henri Konan Bédié, 35 Ans au Service de la Côte d'Ivoire*. Abidjan: Agence Continentale Communication.

Simons, Gary F., and Charles D. Fennig, eds. 2017. *Ethnologue: Languages of the World*. 20th ed. https://www.ethnologue.com/.

Skogseth, Geir. 2006. "Côte d'Ivoire: Ethnicity, *Ivoirité* and Conflict." LandInfo Report, November 26. Accessed May 28, 2017. http://www.landinfo.no/asset/514/1/514_1.pdf.

Smart, Barry. 1993. *Postmodernity*. New York: Routledge.

Smith, Stephen W. 2011. "The Story of Laurent Gbagbo." *London Review of Books* 33 (10): 10–12. http://www.lrb.co.uk/v33/n10/stephen-w-smith/the-story-of-laurent-gbagbo.

Soyinka, Wole. 1996. *The Open Sore of a Continent: A Personal Narrative of the Nigerian Crisis*. New York: Oxford University Press.

———. 2005. *Climate of Fear: The Quest for Dignity in a Dehumanized World*. New York: Random House.

Stearns, Jason K. 2011. *Dancing in the Glory of Monsters: The Collapse of the Congo and the Great War of Africa*. New York: Public Affairs.

Stiglitz, Joseph E. 2002. *Globalization and Its Discontents*. New York: W.W. Norton.

Straus, Scott. 2006. *The Order of Genocide: Race, Power, and War in Rwanda*. Ithaca, NY: Cornell University Press.

Tajfel, Henri, and John Turner. 1979. "An Integrative Theory of Intergroup Conflict." In *The Social Psychology of Intergroup Relations*, edited by William G. Austin and Stephen Worchel, 33–47. Monterey, CA: Brooks/Cole.

Tavares, Pierre Franklin. 2005. *Sur la Crise Ivoirienne: Considérations Éparses; Réflexions sur l'Arraisonnement de la Côte d'Ivoire*. Abidjan: Nouvelles Éditions Ivoiriennes.

Tendler, Judith. 1998. *Good Government in the Tropics*. Baltimore: The Johns Hopkins University Press.

Terreblanche, Sampie. 2002. *A History of Inequality in South Africa: 1650–2002*. Pietermaritzburg, South Africa: University of Natal Press.

Tessilimi, Bakary D. 1984. "Elite Transformation and Political Succession." In *The Political Economy of Ivory Coast*, edited by I. William Zartman and Christopher L. Delgado, 21–55. New York: Praeger.

"Thabo Mbeki Begins Ivory Coast Mediation Mission." 2010. *BBC News*, December 5. http://www.bbc.co.uk/news/world-africa-11920739.

Tiabas, Houlaï Bernard. 2009. *Les Origines de l'instabilité Socio-Politique en Côte d'Ivoire: Des Erreurs Fatales dans la Gestion de L'État de 1959 à 1999*. Côte d'Ivoire: Horizons.

Tocqueville, Alexis de. 2000. *Democracy in America*. Translated, edited, and introduction by Harvey D. Mansfield and Delba Winthrop. Chicago: University of Chicago Press.

Toha, Faustin. 2008. *Devoir de Mensonges: Crise à l'ivoirienne*. Abidjan: NEI-CEDA.

Törnquist, Olle, Neil Webster, and Kristian Stokke, eds. 2009. *Rethinking Popular Representation*. New York: Palgrave Macmillan.

Torres, Camilo. 1968. *Camilo Torres: His Life and His Message: The Text of His Original Platform and All His Messages to the Colombian People*. Edited by John Alvarez García and Christian Restrepo Calle. Translated by Virginia M. O'Grady. Springfield, IL: Templegate Publishers.

Toualy, Georges. 2008. *Le Modèle de Développement Ivoirien: Mirage ou Utopie Partagée?* Paris: L'Harmattan.

Toubabou, Le. 2005. *Le Millefeuille Ivoirien: Un Héritage de Contraintes*. Paris: L'Harmattan.

———. 2011. *Cruelle Côte d'Ivoire: L'elephant et le Machine*. Pars: L'Harmattan.

Toungara, Jeanne Maddox. 2001. "Ethnicity and Political Crisis in Côte d'Ivoire." *Journal of Democracy* 12 (3): 63–72. https://doi.org/10.1353/jod.2001.0059.

Touré, Abdou. 2008. *Alassane Dramane Ouattara: Destin et Liberté*. Saint-Maur-des-Fossés: Sépia.

Touré, Sidi Tiémoko, ed. 2010. *Alassane Dramane Ouattara et les Jeunes: Le Temps des Possibles*. Côte d'Ivoire: Sidi Tiémoko Touré.

Tutu, Desmond. 1999. *No Future without Forgiveness*. New York: Double Day.

United Nations Security Council. 2011a. "Twenty-Ninth Progress Report of the Secretary-General on the United Nations Operation in Côte d'Ivoire." Report S/2011/807*, December 30. http://www.un.org/en/ga/search/view_doc.asp?symbol=S/2011/807.

United Nations Security Council. 2011b. "Twenty-Seventh Progress Report of the Secretary-General on the United Nations Operation in Côte d'Ivoire." Report S/2011/211, March 30. Accessed May 28, 2017. http://www.un.org/en/ga/search/view_doc.asp?symbol=S/2011/211.

USAID. 2012. "HIV/AIDS Health Profile: Sub-Saharan Africa." http://pdf.usaid.gov/pdf_docs/pdacu659.pdf.

Uzokwe, Alfred Obiora. 2003. *Surviving in Biafra: The Story of the Nigerian Civil War: Over Two Million Died*. New York: Writers Advantage.

Vanoutrivel, L. 1977. "Interactionism and Neo-Marxism—A Critical Analysis." *Deviance et Societe* 1 (3): 253–89. https://www.ncjrs.gov/App/publications/Abstract.aspx?Id=60232.

Veblen, Thorstein. 1908. *The Theory of the Leisure Class: An Economic Study of Institutions*. New York: MacMillan.

Vision Reporter. 2012. "I am an Expert in Governance—Museveni." *New Vision: Uganda's Leading Daily*, February 20. Accessed May 28, 2017. http://www.newvision.co.ug/new_vision/news/1299713/expert-governance-museveni.

von Albertini, Rudolph. 1982. *European Colonial Rule, 1880–1940: The Impact of the West on India, Southeast Asia, and Africa*. Translated by J. G. Williamson. Westport, CT: Greenwood Press.

Walzer, Michael. 2009. "A Better Vision: The Idea of Civil Society." In *The Civil Society Reader*, edited by Virginia Ann Hodgkinson and Michael W. Foley, 306–21. London: Tufts University Press.

Wax, Emily. 2003. "For Now, Ivory Coast's Northern Rebels Enjoy Goodwill; Group's Leaders Noted for Civility, if not Governance." *Washington Post*, March 10.

Wehr, Paul. 1979. *Conflict Regulation*. Boulder, CO: Westview Press.

Weiskel, Timothy C. 1980. *French Colonial Rule and the Baule People: Resistance and Collaboration, 1889–1911*. Oxford: Claredon Press.

"Who are Nigeria's Boko Haram Islamists?" 2016. *BBC News*, November 24. http://www.bbc.co.uk/news/world-africa-13809501.

Wilmot, William W., and Joyce L. Hocker. 2007. *Interpersonal Conflict*. 7th ed. New York: McGraw Hill.

World Bank. 2009. *Decentralization and Local Democracy in the World: First Global Report 2008*. Washington, DC: World Bank.

Yaqub, Nuhu. 2007. "The Brain Drain Phenomenon in Nigeria and the Struggles by the Academic Staff Union of Universities (ASUU) to Address It." Paper presented at the Conference of Rectors, Vice-Chancellors and Presidents of African Universities, Zawia, Libya, October 21–27. Accessed May 28, 2017. http://www2.aau.org/corevip07/papers/sec-docs/Yaqub.pdf.

Young, Iris Marion. 1990. *Justice and the Politics of Difference*. Princeton, NJ: Princeton University Press.

———. 2011. *Responsibility for Justice*. Oxford: Oxford University Press.

Zadi Kessy, Marcel. 2004. *Développement de Proximité et Gestion des Communautés Villageoises*. Abidjan: Eburnie.

Zahiri-Ziki, Sébastien. 2006. *Regards sur la Crise Ivoirienne: À la Lumière de la Parole de Dieu*. Abidjan: Éditions OMCI.

Zolberg, Aristide R. 1964. *One-Party Government in the Ivory Coast*. Princeton, NJ: Princeton University Press.

Zouande, Salia F. 2011. "Governance and Democratic Transition in Africa: Understanding 'Ivoirité' and the Ethnicity Challenges to Citizenship and Nation-Building in Côte d'Ivoire." Master's thesis, Howard University.

Index

About the Author

T. Y. Okosun is associate professor of justice studies and African and African American studies at Northeastern Illinois University, Chicago, Illinois.

Lightning Source UK Ltd.
Milton Keynes UK
UKOW04n1136191217
314738UK00008B/396/P

9 781498 566551